Daily Gems of Truth

Daily Gems of Truth

VERA SMITH

Springs

CHRISTIAN
LITERATURE

DAILY GEMS OF TRUTH

ISBN 0-9549225-0-6

Published by
SPRINGS CHRISTIAN LITERATURE
63a Kilvergan Road Lurgan
Co Armagh BT66 6LF
Telephone & Fax 028 3839 2274

Produced by
TH JORDAN LTD
1a Millar Street Belfast
Northern Ireland BT6 8JZ
Telephone 028 9045 0866
www.thjordanltd.com

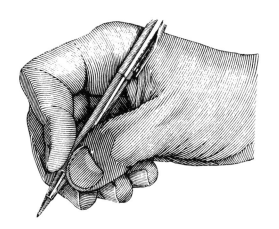

Acknowledgement

I am happy to have a number of dear friends who are talented poets and it is a great joy to publish a few of their poems. I wish to acknowledge the poems contributed by Jean Corbett, Heather Small, Ruth Fullerton, the late Sara McIlveen, and three winners of Springs Poetry Competition, 2000.

Also, the help in proof reading by Daphne Morrow, Eileen and Stanley Trouton: the art and design by Billy Austin, Esther Crawford, Julie-Ann Trouton and the late Ann Magowan

Foreword

I appreciate the privilege of writing this foreword to Miss Vera Smith's 'Daily Gems of Truth'.

Three facets of her life are happily combined in these readings.

Firstly, Miss Smith has a comprehensive and detailed knowledge of Scripture. Shortly after her conversion in her teens she had a clear call to full time Christian service. To prepare herself she went to Emmanuel Bible College, Birkenhead, where whe avidly imbibed the teaching which was thoroughly Bible-based. In addition, since then she has been engaged almost exclusively in ministry and pastoral responsibilities, which have necessitated ongoing study of the Word. In the readings in this book she is essentially opening up significant emphases of the Scripture.

Secondly, Miss Smith has had a wide and varied experience in the Lord's service – in Argentina with the Emmanuel Mission, where she worked with her characteristic enthusiasm for some years before she was reluctantly compelled to return home because of her health; in Portadown, where on recovery she was a temporary but very effective lay Assistant in her home congregation, First Portadown Presbyterian Church; throughout Ireland, where as Co-ordinator of the Irish Evangelistic Band for many years she arranged, supervised and motivated outreach across the land; in Portadown again as lay Visitor; and, wherever she has been located, being drawn irresistibly to young people and under God helping them enormously. In these various spheres she has seen the Lord at work – answering prayer, fulfilling promises, overruling events, transforming lives and ministering abundant grace. In these readings she quotes judiciously from this wealth of experience to illustrate and emphasise her themes.

Thirdly, Miss Smith is by nature artistic. Throughout her life, as time permitted, she has taken delight in writing poetry and prose. At this stage, she is using this gift, developed and refined, to share with others the gems of truth which she herself has found in Scripture.

I have been using these readings daily in their former separate booklet format and I have found them to be searching, humbling, encouraging and inspiring. It is my prayer that the Lord will bless and spiritually enrich the lives of many, of all age groups, who will purchase this book and read it daily.

W. M. Craig

Facing the Future

READING   Joshua 1

As I was with Moses, so I will be with you.
I will never leave you or forsake you.   Joshua 1: 5

*J*oshua faced a daunting task. He had to take the responsibility of leading God's chosen people and following in the footsteps of Moses, the greatest leader the world has ever known. There was the mental fatigue of keeping the great multitude together and working out his strategy... Jordan was ahead and all the territories from the desert and Lebanon to the Euphrates river. All the Hittite country and on to the great sea had to be confronted. (Jos 1: 4) Then there was the physical danger of enemies to be attacked. What a task! No doubt he had fears, but God had made a promise to Joshua, 'I will be with you'.

We may be facing situations that would cause us to fear. There may be rivers to cross, mountains to climb and difficult areas to enter where we will face opposition and danger. We may encounter 'giants' resulting in physical and mental fatigue, but God promises to be with us. Every new beginning presents new opportunities for the child of God to prove that He never breaks a promise. God responds to faith - even faith like a grain of mustard seed will be rewarded! Let us therefore take hold of God's promise and claim His presence, not just for today, but for the future.

He will be with you

He will be with you in sunshine,
He will be with you in shade,
He still keeps His covenant promise
He's **Almighty, Eternal, I am**!
He gave to Moses His promise,
was faithful to him to the end
and He kept His promise to Joshua,
so on God's faithfulness You can depend!

A New Beginning

READING   Philippians 3

Forgetting those things which are behind...I press towards the mark
for the prize of the high calling of God in Christ Jesus.'   Philippians 3: 13 & 14

*S*ince time began, God has been interested in new beginnings. In the beginning, God created the heaven and the earth.   After the flood, through Noah, God made a new beginning. God looked at the plight of His people in Egypt and prepared Moses to deliver His people.

It is interesting to notice throughout the Scriptures the number of times it was necessary for the children of Israel to start again. Although it was not God's will to give His people a king, they requested one and God gave them their desire -the first King was Saul and each succeeding king marked a new beginning. Through the prophets, God gave His people the opportunity to repent and make a fresh start. Finally in the fullness of time, God sent His Son to be the Saviour of the world, thus the whole of mankind entered the dispensation of Grace, with salvation by faith and the free gift of Eternal Life. Time will end with a new beginning, for 'God will create new heavens and a new earth and the former things will not be remembered, nor come to mind'. (Isaiah 65: 17)

Who has not felt the need for a new beginning? There are times when it is necessary to let go of certain memories, hurts and failures and press forward to new goals and hopes. Marie Halter spent twenty years institutionalised in a mental home. She met Joe, married, but shortly afterwards he died. Marie lives today lecturing and helping in the United States of America to upgrade and rehabilitate the mentally handicapped. Her background, insecurity and suppression of her feelings led to her illness, but she had a good brain and, through the love and care of two nurses who saw her as one who would make it, she came through to usefulness and sanity. It was a new beginning for Marie Balter! Aspirations for new beginnings are healthy and give impetus for renewed efforts of devotion and service!

The apostle Paul had such landmarks in his spiritual pilgrimage for he records, 'forgetting those things which are behind, I press towards the prize for the high calling of God in Christ Jesus'.

The beginning of a new month is a good time for us to make a new beginning. Let us mark this milestone by a very positive start and purposefully determine to use every means of grace to achieve new spiritual heights.

As I Am - A Prayer

Lord, take me as I am - Take me as I am!
Guilty, helpless and stained by sin,
Lord, take me as I am!

Lord, fill me as I am - Fill me as I am!
This empty vessel I yield to You,
Lord, fill me as I am!

Lord, use me as I am - Use me as I am!
I want to serve You all my days,
Lord, use me as I am!

The Greatness of God

READING   1 Chronicles 29: 10-20

Sometimes a child can capture the greatness of God through poetry or prose and surprise us as to his understanding of Christian truth. Christopher Irwin, aged nine, winner of Springs Millennium Poetry competition wrote....

Greater than the Dome

The dome is big but God is bigger
The dome is wide but God is wider
The dome is high but God is higher
The dome is strong but God is stronger
The dome lights up Greenwich but
God is the Light of the World.

*T*his poem brings to mind King David's concept of God's greatness in 1 Chronicles chapter twenty-nine. Because King David was a man of war God did not let him build the temple. But he did live to see all the preparations and materials brought for his son, Solomon, to build the temple. It would seem that David's vocabulary is exhausted in what is one of the greatest expressions of man's praise and adoration of His God. He commences with the greatness of God in verse eleven and lists the attributes of God - power, glory, victory and majesty; then focuses on the fact that riches and honour come from God and it is God who makes great and gives strength. What a great God! It is good to remind ourselves that what we have has been given to us by God. We cannot even take the glory for any achievement, any success either academically or financially, any name or title that has been given to us - It is God who gives us the health and the ability! Therefore we give the glory back to Him and thank Him for His greatness and His goodness.

Is your God too small?

The Bible tells how Adam and Eve,
thought God was too small;
The serpent said 'Eat of the tree
then just as big as God you'll be,
your eyes will open and you'll see
That God is too small!

When I think of outer space;
Is your God too small?
Myriads of stars - they planets are;
He holds Jupiter, the Moon and Mars
and even earth we can't call **ours**;
My God is not small!

When I think of God as man;
Is your God too small?
He left heaven - to earth came down;
In human flesh He walked around;
Jesus Christ cannot be bound -
My God is not small!

When I think of God in me,
Is your God too small?
That by His spirit He indwells;
My doubts and fears He comes and quells;
Within my heart a chorus swells,
My God is not small!

Quote:
'God is big enough to create the universe yet small enough to live in my heart'.

A Mother's Influence

READING   Exodus 2: 1-8

*'... Take this child away and nurse him
for me, and I will give you your wages'*   *Exodus 2: 9*

*T*he hand that rocks the cradle rules the world'. *(Quotable quote)*
No one should underestimate the influence of a mother. When God was preparing a leader He overruled the laws passed by a pagan king. Pharaoh had tried by hard work and oppression to thwart the growth of the Israelites, but 'the more they oppressed them the more they multiplied and spread', so the Egyptians came to dread the Israelites (chapter 1:12). The midwives disobeyed the king and did not kill the male Israelites at birth. God would fulfil His purposes and keep His promises to Abraham, Isaac and Jacob - Israel would become a mighty nation. It was into a land where the Jews were hated that baby Moses was born.

Every child who is familiar with the Bible has loved the story of Moses and the bulrushes. A baby born to a couple in the house of Levi gave birth to a darling baby boy. What joy and pleasure and what dread of the law of the land-their baby son would die! The mother devises a plan to hide the child in an effort to save her baby. She got a papyrus basket and coated it with tar and pitch, then placed her precious treasure in the basket and hid him among the reeds along the banks of the River Nile. Miriam, her daughter, would keep watch from a distance and warn her mother of any danger. Pharaoh's daughter went down to the river to bathe and, as she and her attendants walked along the bank of the river, the baby was spotted. When the basket was opened they discovered the little bundle of humanity. Moses was crying. The princess felt sorry for the little one and when Miriam suggested getting a nurse it was agreed. Thus the mother of the child became nurse and was paid by the princess. When the child grew older he was taken to the palace and became heir to the throne of Egypt.

In the providence of God a pagan king was shaping a man for the destiny of a nation, while at the same time God was preparing a man to become the leader of His people. Pharaoh trained God's man for the purpose of the King of Kings and His mother shaped him for his spiritual leadership.

No one or nothing can thwart the plan of God and no one should underestimate the influences of a godly mother.

A New Baby - Congratulations!

No disappointment - just surprise
For you thought you carried a baby boy!
But now that all suspense is past-
your bundle of joy has arrived at last.
Take this little one born today
and lead her to Jesus - the Truth, the Way;
teach her to love the things that are good
- to obey her parents as a good child should;
help her in every way you can
to grow up lending a helping hand
to others in need of a special friend,
who perhaps have a hurt that she can help mend:
teach her to respect the powers that be-
to contribute to peace and sanity,
for we live in a world where family ties
are lost to the sight of the worldly-wise:
now you're the proud mother of a new little life
-you have a mother's heart and you're a faithful wife -
so Judith, I pray for help from the Lord
to bring up this child and teach her God's Word,
for His Word is a light and a lamp to her feet
it will guide her through life, till the Saviour she meets.

(Laura Ruth Loney was born on 4 January 2002)

7

Hard Work Produces a Harvest

READING   Genesis 26

Isaac sowed in that land and received in the same year
one hundredfold, and the Lord blessed him.   Genesis 26: 12

*T*he setting of Genesis 26 is a famine. The Philistines had filled in all the wells that Abraham had dug and Isaac finds himself faced with a challenge - starvation or hard work. God prohibits him from going down into Egypt where there was plenty but told him to stay in the land of promise and He would bless him. There were problems to overcome when the herdsmen of Gerar strove with the herdsmen of Isaac. This resulted in more hard work and more wells had to be dug until there was an agreement with the men of Gerar. At last there was harmony and both parties were content. Isaac pitched his tent in the valley of Gerar and found a well of springing water - God's provision was plentiful - a springing well from which the land could be irrigated. This was the beginning of another phase in the fulfilment of God's promise. Now the seed had to be sown in order to produce a harvest. But they kept going and reaped a harvest.

God promises His children blessing but not without cost. He takes us into His purposes and then shows us the way to fulfil His plan. It sometimes means digging wells that have become clogged in our Christian lives. The apostle Paul exhorts us to 'lay aside the weights and sins' that so easily beset us. Perhaps we need to take stock and ask God to enable us to dig the wells that have become clogged up with the clay of neglect.

Sometimes God allows us to reach 'rock bottom' - a place of famine to discover the things that hinder our spiritual progress. It was when Isaac re-dug the wells that the land became fertile. When we get rid of the weights and sins God's blessing can flow through us to others.

Refreshment

There is rest for the weary-worn traveller today:
Away from the bustle of life's busy way
At the feet of the Saviour
Who trod life's rough road;
At the foot of the Cross -
Just lay down your load!

There is water to drink from -
Oh foot-worn and sad
As you press through this desert
to yon distant land;
You will find an 'Oasis'
prepared by the Lord;
Just fix your eyes firmly on
Christ through His Word.

Remember How He Led You

READING   Deuteronomy 8

And you shall remember
that the Lord your God led you all the way...   *Deuteronomy 8: 2*

At first Moses had led the children of Israel reluctantly because he felt he was not able for such a task. When he had experience, despite their disobedience, he led them through the wilderness with remarkable skill. In this chapter he asks them to remember that the Lord had led them all the way. His provision had been remarkable - although they suffered hunger, God provided manna, despite their poverty, their clothes did not wear out and God supplied their needs in this way.   How good is our God in looking after our temporal needs. He has promised that 'He will never see the righteous forsaken nor his seed begging bread.' Many can testify to this fact. They may have been tested, but God has either answered by giving them the physical and mental ability to work or, in a marked deliverance, has provided for them.

Think of an instance in your life when God has significantly answered your prayers and provided for you. Remember His goodness and give Him thanks. The God of the past is the God of the present and future - He will not fail you!

God is Faithful

Faithful to His promise
God's Word will ever stand.
Man cannot change one letter
of what His law demands.
If He has promised blessing,
then blessing is secured.
For not one jot or tittle
will Satan ever change.
Our God has deigned to give us
the very best in life,
despite the fiery trials,
in love He thinks is best.
Faithful to His promise,
- the rainbow does appear
as a sign from God in heaven
that we should have no fear
of dark clouds hovering o'er us
to hide the sun from view
for just around the corner
is something bright and new.

Full Surrender

READING   Romans 12

I beseech you therefore brethren, by the mercies of God,
that you present your bodies a living sacrifice, holy,
acceptable to God which is your reasonable service.   *Romans 12: 1*

If Jesus is God

If Jesus is God and died in my place
then all that I give Him has been given by grace:
I have no merit or right of my own
to enter His presence and approach His throne.
If Jesus is God I surrender my will
and ask for His mercy and trust Him to fill
all of my being with His divine power
till self will be conquered and His beauty flower!

*W*riting to the Christians at Rome, Paul first of all makes a plea to them and then reasons with them as to why they should surrender. To fight for one's own rights is the norm but the Christian must learn that the secret of victory in the Christian life is surrender. It does not mean weakness, in fact, some of the most spiritual and dedicated men of history were men of character and backbone! But the Lordship of Christ means our submission to Him results in strength to fight the Lord's battles with the right motives and attitudes. Someone has aptly said, 'any jellyfish can go with the stream but it takes backbone to go against it'. Let us be those who will 'speak the truth in love', but also those who 'will not let the world squeeze us into its mould' (J B Philips).

In his two volumes, 'The Man who Changed the World', Hebert Lockyer takes us through history highlighting the characteristics of those who have made the most impact on our world. It is noteworthy how many of them were totally surrendered to the Lordship of Jesus Christ. The apostle Paul challenged the church at Rome and his message is unchanged today - surrender is the only way to freedom!

Fruit-Bearing in Old Age

READING   Psalm 92

The righteous shall flourish like a palm tree…
They shall still bear fruit in old age;'   *Psalm 92: 12 & 14*

*O*ld age can be frightening for some. The fear of sickness, senility, immobility, poverty, rejection and loneliness robs the mind of poise and tranquillity. There are many promises for old age in the scriptures. The most unexpected promise is that of fruitfulness. Since the age of childbearing is past for a woman and weariness because of hard work can occupy the thoughts of males, producing becomes a memory.   Society places such importance on younger people, that many have adjusted to a negative approach to the eventide of life and look at the 'declining years' with a wrong attitude. The scriptures do not teach us to fear old age, but rather to look on it as a time of development and enjoyment.

In this beautiful poetic psalm David tells us that the righteous shall flourish like the palm tree. Palm trees are noted for their durability - they are evergreens and can offer splendid shade in tropical countries. Unlike most other trees, the palm tree's roots go down deep into the earth. While other trees die in severe drought the palm tree will stand because its roots go deeper in search of water. The Christian who learns the secret of setting the roots of his life into God will stand the drought of old age.

Not only is the righteous like the palm tree but he grows like the cedars in Lebanon. Those cedars we are told are the most stately of all cedars. There is no need for the elderly saint to droop spiritually, for ample provision has been made for victory at all stages of life including old age. Make sure that fruitfulness marks the final years of life's pilgrimage and, if your health does not permit outside activities, use your time wisely to pray and encourage others in their pilgrimage heavenward.

Autumn

When God chose the colours of autumn
He majored in shades of rich gold
to remind us of eternal glories
in a land where we never grow old!
God knew that the earth needed colour,
ere stripped of her foliage to die
so He added rust, yellow and orange
- mixed tones that would catch every eye!

How good is the God of creation
in selecting colours so fair
that would blend with earth's natural greenness
and give autumn vistas more rare!
If He pays such attention to nature
to prepare for the darkness and cold,
there need never be fear of life's winter -
God gives colour despite growing old!

'Even to your old age.... I will carry, and will deliver you'
Isaiah 46: 4

An Empty World

READING   Jeremiah 31: 1-19

I have loved you with an everlasting love,
therefore with loving kindness I have drawn you.   *Jeremiah 31: 3*

*A*lthough the book of Jeremiah is a book of doom, we marvel at the mercy of God to a wayward and disobedient people. In chapter nine Jeremiah cries, 'Oh that my head were waters, and my eyes a fountain of tears, that I might weep day and night for the slain of the daughters of my people' and in chapter thirty-one he pours in the balm of healing by reminding Israel that God has loved them with an everlasting love. We are condemned with no place of refuge other than the arms of a forgiving, loving heavenly Father. God's love is unconditional. We do not need to offer excuses for He already knows our failure. All He requires is a genuine repentance and promises that, if we confess our sins, He is faithful and just to forgive us our sins and to cleanse us from all unrighteousness'. Because He is holy, He demands sorrow for sin and true repentance. Are you feeling rejected today'? Have you failed your Lord and feel there is no way back? There is a way back to your first love because God's love is unconditional and He will receive you. He has loved you with an everlasting love.

Nothing to Offer

The world has nothing to offer the man who is torn by fear
but torment and pain and misery as guilt his conscience sears:
God has something to offer with His pardon, peace and love
and He beckons the weary sinner with mercy from above:
He calls us to His presence with all our sin and woe,
then sends us out to witness - and not one cent we owe!
How wonderful this mercy to every sinner's ears!
God's love surpasses knowledge as He dries the falling tears.
Oh God we can't repay You for all that You have done
but we accept the offer of pardon through Your Son!

14

God Keeps His Promise

READING   Genesis 9: 1-17

I set My rainbow in the cloud, and it shall be
for the sign of the covenant between Me and the earth.   *Genesis 9: 13*

We look back in history and read about the rainbow and we look up when the rainbow appears and thank God for His faithfulness.

There never had been a flood on the earth, but in obedience Noah set to work and constructed a boat on dry land for he believed God would destroy the earth with a flood. It happened just as God had told Noah.

This is a beautiful story for children, but what a truth for all of us. God never breaks a promise.

Kathryn Mawhinney, aged fourteen, prize winner of 'A Poem for the Millennium', writes about the ark.

Rainbow

God sent His word to Noah
'The world is being bad
Ignoring my commandments
This really makes me sad.'

God said, 'Noah you're my friend
Please build a wooden ark.
Hurry Noah, time is short
The sky is getting dark.

Along with all your family
Put two of every kind
Of bird and fish and animal
All, which you must find.'

Other people laughed at him
To build a boat inland.
'Oh well,' said Noah, 'I trust in God
I have His helping hand.'

When the work was finished
The thunderstorms began.
The people cried to Noah
'Please save us if you can!'

The rainstorm had just ended
The sun came out to dry.
The earth no more had puddles,
The clouds no more will cry.

Noah and the animals
They left the wooden boat.
On solid ground they now could walk
No longer had to float.

God then promised Noah
He never would again
Flood the earth completely
With such torrential rain.

To remind us of this promise
To Noah, you and I
When it rains through sunshine
A rainbow fills the sky.

Bonds of Fellowship

READING   Psalm 103

He made known his ways to Moses,
his acts to the children of Israel.   Psalm 103: 7

*G*od wants to share His secrets with His children. Because He knows what we are capable of achieving and knows what is best for us, and because He has an eternal purpose, He brings us into situations where we discover there is a plan in the seemingly uneventful events of life. But we must halt in our ceaseless activity to discover the plan. Sometimes we are afraid to let go of our ambitious plans to allow God to interrupt the course of life and show us His better plan. At the 'burning bush' Moses experienced a divine intervention into an ordinary situation, doing an ordinary job. God broke into the life of Moses. He was looking after his father-in-law's sheep at the far side of the desert when he was arrested by something unusual. What he saw was an ordinary bush, but it burned and, as he kept on looking, it continued to burn. God got the attention of Moses and as he came near to see such a spectacular sight, God called to him, 'Moses! Moses!'

Often God is trying to get our attention and take us into His purpose for our lives, but we are not tuned in to hear His voice. He tries various ways of distracting us. Sometimes it is the obvious and ordinary - a simple interruption in the course of normal duty! But we fail to recognise it and carry on without turning aside. Then He sometimes comes in the spectacular - a disappointment, failure, hurt, or even a bereavement. It is much more acceptable to learn the lessons He wants to teach us through the ordinary circumstances of life than to hear His voice through the more drastic interventions. However we hear and recognise God, his interruptions are for our good - He has a better and eternal purpose and wants to bring us into His confidence for our spiritual benefit. He wants to make known HIS WAYS!

Quote:
'Man's chief end is to glorify God and to enjoy Him for ever.'

A Desolate Seashore

I walked along a seashore,
one blustery autumn night,
battling with the Saviour
about walking in the light.
My plans I showed Him plainly
would bring me wealth and ease
-Why should I be so lonely,
I had myself to please?
He told me of the purpose
He had to reach the lost
-That man's salvation cost Him
Gethsemane and the cross.

I walked along a seashore
one peaceful autumn night,
talking with the Saviour
about promises so bright.
His plans, I saw so clearly,
were better than my own
for wealth and ease can never
bring happiness, make a home!
I told God of the pleasure
I had in serving Him
-Now my memory is my treasure
of service for my King!

Encouragement

READING   Romans 15

For whatever things were written before
were written for our learning, that we through the patience
and comfort of the Scriptures might have hope.   Romans 15: 4

*W*hy read the Scriptures daily?   Surely it can become a routine and 'familiarity breeds contempt', someone might comment. God's Word is powerful - it is the living word and not like any other book. It is our daily food and, just as we need nourishment to grow physically, we need to feed 'the inner man' to grow and develop spiritually. God has provided the right nourishment and without it we shrivel up spiritually.

Pray before reading and ask God, through His Spirit, to reveal fresh nuggets of truth. Then when you read you will receive encouragement from the Scriptures.

Paul wrote this in the context of strong Christians being tolerant of the failings of the weak, and helping them rather than pleasing themselves. God wants us to be those who will inspire other believers in their Christian faith. We can do this by genuine friendship and words of encouragement, but the greatest and most permanent boost we can give to a fellow believer is to use the Scriptures as we exercise 'the gift of encouragement'. God's Word will live long after we have left!

Encourage - that's God's way!

It only takes a little word -
a smile, a shake of hand
to help another on life's way,
perhaps lighten someone's load:

The world is full of lonely folk
who bravely face the world
but hide behind a smiling face
a cross, a heavy load!

So you could be the one to cheer,
To brighten someone's day -
Haste then, some little kindness show;
Encourage - That's God's way!

On the Potter's Wheel

READING   Jeremiah 18

And the vessel that he made of clay was marred
in the hand of the potter; so he made it again
into another vessel as it seemed good to the potter to make.   Jeremiah 18: 4

God sometimes has to take us aside to show us things in our lives that are not pleasing to Him. It is not a pleasant experience and can be quite painful. It may be the wounds of another that have taken root and turned sour. God does not want us to harbour hurt and, because He is preparing us for His holy heaven, He has the right to work in every area of our lives. He shakes us up and gently points out His displeasures with us, then it's back to the potter's house where the vessel has to be remade. It hurts!

Very often when He does take the time to bring us fresh revelation of His holiness it comes as a shock because we discover how far short we are of His standards. There are some ugly warts and we are not at all pleased with the discovery. But we soon realise that it is for our good and allow the Potter to do what He wants with the clay.

A New Vessel

Marred by the words of another,
Left wounded and bitter inside -
No healing I found where I sought it;
In self-pity I grovelled around
till along came the Master designer,
picked up all the pieces He found
then moulded and fashioned a vessel
with the purpose He had in mind.
He took even the smallest fragments
back to the Potter's house
to be melted and shaped as seemed fitting
for a vessel of exquisite design..

The Saviour's Voice

READING   1 Samuel 3

Speak Lord, for Your servant hears.   1 Samuel 3: 9

*I*t is possible to listen and not hear! No doubt we have all been guilty of not listening to someone and leaving without having heard.

This is all too common when we have our 'quiet time'. Have you ever left the 'quiet place' disappointed that you have been too rushed to hear God's voice? You have read the scriptures and thought on the contents of the passage but you have failed to hear God's voice.

God wants to communicate His plans to us. He has a great purpose for our lives in His overall plan for the world. If we do not hear, we will miss being His instruments in what He is doing. God's purposes will not be thwarted but we will be the losers. It is only as we hear His words of strength, comfort, peace and blessing and keep in tune with Him that we can go out to fulfil His will for our lives. Revelation is the result of hearing the Saviour's voice!

The Saviour's Voice

The Saviour's voice it is so sweet,
it gives me strength when I am weak;
His words of comfort thrill my soul -
'My child fear not, I make you whole.'

The Saviour's voice, it whispers peace
as to my soul there comes release.
From all the stress of life he frees
and blesses me while on my knees.

The Saviour's voice, it tells the way
to those who take the time to pray;
The weary traveller finds repose,
The way ahead he lets Christ choose.

The Saviour's voice, it reassures
a 'doubting Thomas' filled with fears;
He conquered death when He arose
and triumphed over every foe.

The Saviour's voice, it calls me 'Come'
to heaven my final rest and Home
- where I shall be for ever near
the One whose voice I learned to hear.

My Father's World

READING   John 14

FOR MEDITATION: 'In my Father's house
are many mansions - I go to prepare a place for you.
And if I go and prepare a place for you, I will come again
and receive you to myself; that where I am there you may be also.'   *John 14: 2 & 3*

*I*n 1996 I visited the OMS headquarters in Greenwood, Indiana. Our group had a special treat - we were taken to a parkland owned by a friend of OMS, called 'My Father's World'. It was a dream world, reminding me of a paradise somewhere between the Biblical description of Eden and heaven! As I stole away to a place of solitude beside a lake, I thought - 'If a man-made place can be so beautiful, what must heaven be like!

When we drove into 'My Father's World', we were taken to a quaint American homestead. Flags of different nations were flying outside, reminding us of God's heart of love for a lost world. Then we entered the house, where we were allowed to wander around leisurely. We went back in history to a way of life, long forgotten in modern America, but the norm for the early settlers in the New World. Old lamps and antiques fascinated me!

Then, it was outside into the fresh air and bright June sunshine to enjoy the quietness and beauty of an extensive parkland with flowers, shrubs and trees beautifully landscaped for the enjoyment and relaxation of guests. I found a delightful spot overlooking a lake and wrote my poem - 'My Father's World'.

This visit to 'My Father's World' is a memory to be treasured for days when skies were grey.

Every day can be treasured as we realise that God has given us life to enjoy and a world filled with reminders of His creation. It is ours to enjoy! Unfortunately, sin has marred our vision and some days pass with memories of an unhappy childhood, a wasted youth and a life that goes past with the negative feelings and impressions of the past. The positive blessings can become skeletons in the cupboards of despair!

You can change things! Go out into the future to rejoice in God's love, see the beauty of His creation. Take opportunities to do good and make sure that you enjoy.
Our Father's World!

My Father's World

In my Father's World, I see His mighty hand
making tiny flowers to decorate the land:
Every blade of grass, various shapes of leaves;
hues of natural colour, God blends with perfect ease:
He gives His children pleasure, takes away the stress and strain
refreshes mind and body - gives goals for which to aim.

In my Father's World, I see His matchless love
providing for the sinner salvation for the soul;
The trees, they speak of Calvary, the leaves they whisper peace;
The stillness brings its healing and to the mind release;
God's love for all His children, so clearly can be seen
when we get alone with nature and breathe in air that's clean.

In my Father's World, I see His mission heart
yearning for the nations, of His family to be a part:
and so my eyes would focus on a world that's lost in sin,
endeavouring the Gospel across the world to bring,
that some from every nation - north, south, east and west -
will be for ever happy in God's eternal rest.

The Work and Effect of Righteousness

READING   Isaiah 32

The work of righteousness will be peace,
and the effect of righteousness, quietness and assurance forever.   Isaiah 32: 17

*L*ike a calm river making its way through a parched land, causing the trees and flowers to spring to life, so the peace of God flows into our lives, cleansing the soul and healing the scars of hurt inflicted by a world where love is not the hallmark. It is only God's peace that gives quietness and assurance and causes its effects to bring blessing to others.

While touring in Scotland with a friend one blustery September day, we travelled from John O'Groats, along the north coast, stopping at Dunnet Head.   The gale force winds sent those Atlantic breakers crashing against the rugged cliffs sending gallons of water rocketing upwards. They thundered as they crashed, and helplessly dropped back into the sea! Ships dived into the depths, emerging with stern reaching towards the sky, as if crying to the Almighty for mercy. It was invigorating but frightening. We left the scene sensing some of man's inability to control the elements. One could only feel sympathy with the multitude of tormented people crashing hopelessly on the waves of life without a guide and without hope at the end of the journey. We continued our journey towards Tongue. Some miles east of Tongue we decided to change direction and follow the road along the Navar River. As we toured south through some of Scotland's most picturesque scenery, the river meandered through sweet hedgerows, washing boulders and fallen trees in its relentless flow to the great ocean. There was no sense of hurry as in places her shallow water trickled over stones and small pebbles, her gurgles breathing peace and tranquillity.

Dews of Quietness

Lord, take from me the
strain and stress
of hurrying to and fro;
then give to me serenity
that from my life may flow
a living stream of water clear
dispelling doubt and fear
and making life a symphony
of music to the ear!

Getting our Priorities Right

READING   Psalm 37

Rest in the Lord, and wait patiently for Him:
do not fret because of him who prospers in his way...   Psalm 37: 7

*A*s we journey through life there are times when we are tempted to look at others and feel that their lot is easier than our own. If we knew the pressures of the other person we might change our mind! But certainly if the devil can succeed in making us discontented with our lot in life we can lose our peace. God has to deal with us and bring us back to a place of 'soul rest', where we regain our poise and get our priorities right.

I have found, and others have testified also, that a good way to do this is to read a psalm of David. In Psalm 37 we are exhorted 'Fret not because of evil-doers'; 'Trust in the Lord': 'Delight in the Lord'; 'Commit our way unto the Lord; trust also in Him' and 'Rest in the Lord.' Reflecting on the first seven verses of this psalm I see the futility of setting my standards by those around me and I rise to focus on the positive results of trusting in the Lord, delighting in the Lord, and committing my way to Him.

Refresh my Soul in God

I want to bask in Your presence Lord, and feel Your cleansing power:
I want to find Your peace and love and rest beneath your bower:
for everywhere I hear the noise of voices that cause me to fear
and lose the sense of Your presence and the feeling that You are near.

I want to walk with You by day and hear Your voice speak 'peace':
I want to lay me down at night as Your Spirit brings release:
for the call of the world seems urgent with demands from here and there
till it seems the place of duty is 'my all' I have to share.

I want to know the quietness of God's promised 'rest of soul':
I want fresh revelation that makes me feel 'I'm whole':
Without God's touch I'm empty, without His joy I'm sad
and life is not worth living, if I lose the peace I had!

Draw near to God and He will draw near to you.

Can God Use Me?

READING   John 6: 1-14

There is a lad here who has five barley loaves,
and two small fish: but what are they among so many.   *John 16: 9*

*C*an God use me? I do not have much to offer Him. I do not have gifts like other people and I feel insignificant in a society that gives opportunity to people with outstanding abilities. Yes, God has a special job for you! He wants to take you just as you are and use you for His glory. John gives us a very special detail in the story of the feeding of the five thousand. It is the provision of five barley loaves and two small fish by **a lad.** Who would have thought that a small lunch given by a boy could have resulted in a miracle?   Even the disciples must have been amazed when Jesus told them to make the people sit down. What would happen? The Master took the loaves, gave thanks and then distributed them to the disciples to distribute to the multitude - likewise with the fish. How astonishing when the disciples gathered up twelve baskets full of the remains of the five barley loaves after everyone was fed. God took what little the boy had - five barley loaves and two small fish - and multiplied it to feed the multitude. He still does the same. He takes the gifts we offer Him to feed the spiritually hungry.

A Little Lunch

A little lad was wandering
Beside the lake one day,
When through the crowds of people
Someone was heard to say...

Has anybody brought a lunch?
The Master calls for food!
Then suddenly his bag of bread
And fishes smelled so good!

Those tasty fish would be too small
To slice or chop or carve;
And if he gave the loaves away
Then he himself would starve!

But children faint around him
Were crying to be fed;
How could he hide his picnic
When families needed bread?

And so he gave it willingly,
That evening on the shore;
So God could work a miracle
And feed so many more.

Those loaves and fishes multiplied
Five thousand times at least
That the humble little snack
Became a mighty feast!

And so it is with you and me,
Our lives are like that lunch,
So little, when they're brought to God,
But in His hand, so much.

Alison Brown, winner of Springs Millennium Poetry Competition.

Remember God in Your Youth

READING   Ecclesiastes 12

Remember now your Creator in the days of your youth…   *Ecclesiates 12: 1*

*L*ife is a journey from the cradle to the grave and every milestone is significant in our development. Childhood is such a happy, carefree season when we discover, explore and just enjoy the pleasure of living without any responsibilities. All too soon these years pass and we emerge into our teens with all the physical and psychological changes shaking our confidence while at the same time producing a sense of independence.

Youth is the time of mental development and agility. No doubt it is because of this that we are exhorted to 'remember our Creator'. It is significant that most people come to faith in Jesus Christ in their teens.

Remember you were made in God's image and created to have fellowship with your Maker. - Give Him your best! Go into the future with your hand firmly in His and He will be your Guide, your Friend and Helper.

A Dream of Heaven

When I was only six or seven,
I had a lovely dream of heaven.
The Saviour called to me to come -
said, 'Child, I want to take you Home!'
Two angels stood above my head -
they lifted me from off the bed!
As up we soared to realms of light,
the pearly gates appeared in sight:
We entered to a trumpet sound,
then happy faces did resound:
I walked on streets of solid gold ,
met Abraham and men of old
who welcomed me with outstretched arms,
told me of heaven's holy charm!

I saw the walls of jasper bright -
they dazzled in the heavenly light!
When I approached the Throne of God,
On bended knee, I whispered, 'LORD'!
 'I know you child - you know My Son',
take now the Crown of Life, you've won!'
I took my prize, and bowed my head:
then I awoke - I was in bed!
That dream has robbed death of its sting -
the praises of my Lord I'll sing
until I gaze upon His face
and thank Him for His Saving Grace!

Worship the Christ
Of the Emmaus Road

READING   24: 13-49

'...Jesus Himself drew near and went with them.'   Luke 24: 15

*T*he meeting with the risen Christ in a house in Emmaus would be an experience never to be forgotten. Jesus had indicated to Cleophas and his friend as they walked on the Emmaus road that He was going farther, but they constrained Him -

Luke 24: 29.'Abide with us, for it is towards evening, and the day is far spent.'

He accepted their invitation and the next scene portrayed for us by Luke is the 'Breaking of Bread' in a house in Emmaus. (It is interesting to note that although the Lord's Supper was instituted in The Upper Room, the first Lord's Supper was celebrated by our Lord Himself in a home in the village of Emmaus!) Was this the home of one of the two? Were there others present when they entered the house? These details are not given, but we can picture the scene.

'Now it came to pass, as He sat at the table with them, that He took bread, blessed and broke it, and gave it to them.

'Then their eyes were opened and they knew Him; and He vanished from their sight.' Luke 24: 31.

The disciples summed up this meeting at the home in Emmaus, with the immortal words - 'Did not our hearts burn within us...' Luke 24: 32. These words have been used by generations of Bible teachers and preachers for over two thousand years. The great John Wesley, founder of Methodism, spoke of his new birth experience in, as the 'Burning Heart'.

What would the disciples do now? Luke makes sure his readers would note the urgency of their encounter with the Risen Lord on the road and in the village of Emmaus, and records -   'So they rose up that very hour and returned to Jerusalem, and found the eleven and those who were with them gathered together.' Luke 24: 33.

When they reached Jerusalem they found the others. Were they in the large Upper Room used for the institution of the Lord's Supper? We do not know but they were gathered together and they too were discussing the appearance of the Lord Jesus Christ and confirmed that He had appeared to Simon Peter. We can imagine their joy as the Emmaus disciples told of their encounter with the Risen Saviour!

As they rejoiced in what had happened, suddenly the Risen Christ appears!

'Now as they said these things, Jesus Himself stood in the midst of them, and said to them, 'Peace to you.'
But they were terrified and frightened, and supposed they had seen a spirit.' Luke 24: 36-37.

Through fear and consternation, the disciples were dumb founded, but He reassured them and invited them to look at His hands and feet and see for themselves that He was indeed the same Jesus who had been crucified. Again, He confirmed from the Old Testament scriptures, the prophecies concerning the event. Luke records the fact that He used the 'law of Moses , the Prophets and the Psalms' on the road to Emmaus, and we know that in Jerusalem, He again used the 'Book of Psalms', as well as the 'Law of Moses and the Prophets'. He also assured them of the coming of the Holy Spirit, the third Person of the Trinity, whom the Father would send when He would return to heaven.

The outcome of this encounter was enlightenment, resulting in joy and praise. Later, of course, the eyes of their spiritual understanding were opened to the full revelation, when the Holy Spirit was outpoured at Pentecost.

I had the privilege of walking in the footsteps of the two disciples who were joined by the risen Christ and, although I did not have the physical presence of the Son of God, I experienced His presence, in the third person of the trinity - the Holy Spirit...

Christ is King

Do not cry; O do not cry;
Although the Saviour is to die;
Weep no more; O weep no more
for He will open Heaven's door!
Sigh no more; O do not sigh
behold redemption draweth nigh!
Jesus will the victory win
- Over sin!

Lift your eyes; O lift your eyes;
'It is finished!' The Saviour cried
He arose; O He arose!
He triumphed over all His foes;
Joy at last; O joy at last!
The curse and wrath of God are past;
Sin and death have lost their sting
- Christ is King!

Love

READING   1 Corinthians 13

And now abide faith, hope, love,
these three; but the greatest of these is love.   *1 Corinthians 13: 13*

A World Without Love

Can you imagine a world without books,
man groping in darkness - vacant his look?
Affected by trifles, through eye and through ear,
then inner confusion as he battles with fear:
a quest for knowledge but nowhere to find
a library of books to bring light to the mind,
great hidden discoveries, lost to our race,
events that made history - nobody can trace!
No works of Shakespeare, Dickens or Yeats,
historic battles, no trace of their dates,
for great schools of learning have no books to teach
- all figures and facts have been passed down in speech!

Can you imagine a world without friends,
just 'greetings' and 'farewells' - beginning and end?
- Each person an island within himself,
toiling and slaving for gain and great wealth;
no satisfaction of giving a gift,
or sharing life's problems, till some burden will lift,
talking together of times when we cried,
laughing and joking o'er joys we can't hide!

Can you imagine a world without trees,
impoverished the landscape without branches and leaves?
Our homes stripped of items carved from rich wood
- no dark polished table that makes food look good!
Think of the uses of wood in the world -
it's worth must be valued like silver and gold!
a carpenter's bench and noise of a saw,
his job satisfaction, admiring with awe
a table, a chair, framed great works of art
- even tools that he used have wood in some part!
I cannot imagine a world without trees -
no wood to make ships to plough through rough seas;
no thrill to discover some far distant land -
for Pitt and 'the fathers' no wood for their hands
to skilfully build their houses and barns
and plant England's image on American sands!

Can you imagine a world without love -
no family unit protecting the brood?
Children like orphans roaming the streets,
fighting and cursing the young folks they meet;
no bonds of friendship enriching the life,
no deeds of kindness - just hatred and strife;
man void of feeling - a shell without soul,
selfish ambition out of control;
anger like cancer devouring the cells;
hatred and murder making life a hell.
The thought of a world without actions of love -
people fighting for rights as they push and shove
to get to the top in their mad rush for wealth,
not even aware of the damage to health -
makes life so pointless and empty and drear
and our enemy death something to fear!
But God, in His wisdom, placed love in the heart
for life to have meaning, love must be a part
of everyday living with family and friends
- God shows His love in the blessings He sends!

Failure is Not Final

READING   John 18: 15-27 & John 21: 15-19

Jesus said to Simon Peter, "Simon, son of Jonas,
do you love Me more than these?" He said to Him, "Yes, Lord:
You know that I love You." He said to him, "Feed My lambs."   *John 21: 15*

*W*ho would have imagined that Peter would have failed His Lord'? When he first left his fishing nets and with the others set out to be a true disciple Peter had been determined to follow. He had left his fishing boat and walked towards Jesus on the waves - What trust! What faith! But in the hour of testing Peter failed. It must have been a sad moment for him when the 'cock crowed' and he remembered the words of Jesus. Was Peter finished? Of course not.

Chapter twenty-one of John opens with a new daybreak. Jesus was on the shore, and Peter was there when He said, 'Children, have you any meat?' Nothing could have been more welcome to Peter. I can almost imagine him going over the words as he obeyed Jesus by casting his net on the right side of the boat. Then it was Peter who spoke and said, 'It is the Lord.' That discourse after the meal was something which changed Peter's whole future. From failure and disgrace he goes out to become one of the greatest soul-winners ever!

Have you failed? The good news today is that there is hope, and failure need not be final. It was final for Judas but it was the beginning of great things for Peter. Come back in repentance and faith and go out to show the world that there is forgiveness at the cross.

Fragments and Tears

I stepped out of failure
Into success,
Just by acknowledging
That God's ways are best:
I gave Him the fragments
Of life's broken plans;
My bottle of tear-drops
I placed in His hands:
He took what I offered -
Mixed fragments with tears:
Then gave me tranquillity -
The antidote for fear!

I stepped out of failure
Into success:
Aware of a purpose
And deep inner rest:
My life's broken fragments,
The bottle of tears,
The Potter had used
In His purpose to cheer:
He re-made the vessel -
Took out much of 'self':
To reveal His glory-
He filled with Himself!

Gone, But Not Forgotten

READING   John 14: 1-11

For me to live is Christ, and to die is gain.   *Philippians 1: 21*

*M*any who read this will have known heartache. However young or old you are there is sorrow in your life because of a dear one who has gone to heaven, perhaps a grandmother, a father or mother, a brother or sister, a husband or wife, a niece or nephew, or some other close friend. Kind friends offer you sympathy and they feel they may understand, but deep within you are saying, 'They don't really understand my pain.' Time has passed and you thought time would bring healing but instead the pain seems greater.

I hope it brings you comfort to know that for your loved one 'it is gain.' He or she is out of all the discomfort of a terminal illness, a stroke or just the frailty of the ageing process and it is freedom and release. The loss is ours. We miss their words of cheer, their love and thoughtfulness - there is a big ache in our heart which we feel nothing can fill. God understands your heartache so ask Him to fill your heart with His love and pour in 'the oil of joy for mourning and the garment of praise for the spirit of heaviness.'

Gone Home

Gone to his/her dear Saviour,
-for ever now to be
in His immediate presence
from sin and sorrow free:
We'll miss the friendly welcome,
the words of hope and cheer,
but memories we will treasure
of one whom we hold dear.

Gone home - we're sad and lonely:
- no smile, no words of cheer!
no thoughtful card or present -
brings us pain, and oft a tear!
But there's a bright tomorrow
on heaven's golden shore
once more we'll be together
with Christ for evermore!

Measuring Spiritual Maturity

READING   Ephesians 4

Till we come to the unity of the faith,
and of the knowledge of the Son of God, unto a perfect man,
unto the measure of the stature of the fullness of Christ.   *Ephesians 4: 13*

*G*rowing up spiritually can be painful. Paul teaches us that to develop patience and endurance there must be trials and testing - that is not something we relish! But we see through Ephesians chapter 4 that growth is in God's plan for us as individuals and for His church. It is something to which we should apply our minds in order to understand how we can best achieve the goal of attaining God's standards.

God was supremely interested in growth for His people from the beginning of time. In Deuteronomy chapter five He exhorts them to fear Him and keep all His commandments always, that it might be well with them, and with their children for ever. Obedience is the gateway to spiritual growth, and the development of Christian character will have its effect on the next generation, because righteousness is rewarded.

The Lord Jesus reiterated the greatest commandment given to the children of Israel to love the Lord our God with all our heart, soul, mind and strength and our neighbour as ourselves. Bernard of Clairvaux, mystic, hymn writer and theologian said, 'We know God only as far as we love Him,' so we conclude that spiritual maturity comes through obedience to the commands of God and love of God Himself.

Love between two people can be expressed in two ways - by silent communication and understanding of each other, where no words or gestures are necessary, which is a result of a deep appreciation and respect for each other. Secondly, love can be expressed in words and deeds. In the spiritual realm this is worship and adoration coupled with verbal testimony and works that reveal where our loyalties lie.

When it comes to service, the only motive is love. We serve Him because love constrains us. Every true Christian wants to grow and the only place to grow is at the feet of Jesus.

At Jesus' Feet

At Jesus' feet
Love yields her mind -
Eternal Truth
In Him to find.   Luke 10: 39

At Jesus' feet
Love lays her heart -
When hope has gone
That faith may start.   John 11: 32

At Jesus' feet
Love longs to give -
Her life to death,
That Love may live.   John 12: 3-7

Jean Corbett

Quote:
'God builds beautiful creations from ruins.'

He Will Be Remembered

READING   John 1

Behold the Lamb of God who takes away the sin of the world.   John 1: 29

*E*ven a casual reading of the Bible shows us that when God wanted to carry out His purposes He chose a man, or in certain instances, a woman. To start a nation He chose Abraham, Isaac and Jacob. To lead the children of Israel He chose Moses and, after the death of Moses He chose Joshua. To build the temple He chose Solomon. To save His people he chose Esther. To restore Jerusalem he chose Nehemiah. To prepare for the greatest event in history He chose John the Baptist.

John had a special mission to herald the coming of the Lord Jesus Christ to commence His earthly ministry. John was a most unlikely person. He was a rugged man from the wilderness but God had a purpose for John to accomplish - He was sent from God! When questioned he used the words of Isaiah thus fulfilling the prophecy, 'The voice of one crying in the wilderness; Make straight the way of the Lord.' In disclosing his own identity and pointing to the coming of the Messiah, he confessed that he was not the Christ, but was sent to bear witness of the True Light whom the Jews rejected. When he saw Jesus coming he uttered these immortal words -
'Behold the Lamb of God who takes away the sin of the world.'

After the baptism of Jesus, John fades from the scene - He had his work accomplished. Tragically his end was a sad one, he was beheaded, but he will be remembered for his words... 'behold the Lamb of God who takes away the sin of the world'.
How do we want to be remembered?

Behold the Lamb

Men go down in history for deeds old and new,
Let me be remembered as faithful to You!
The God Who was Alpha before time began
sent Jesus the Saviour to reveal His plan:
sent John as a forerunner, preparing the way,
told him to baptise men who for forgiveness did pray
John now is remembered in jubilant psalm
for words now immortal, **'Behold the Lamb!'**

Dealing With Hurt

READING   Isaiah 53

He was despised and rejected of men,
a man of sorrows and acquainted with grief...   *Isaiah 53: 3*

*M*ost of us have been hurt by others and have known pain and inner suffering as a result. It is not easy to accept hurt, particularly if you know you were not the guilty party. Working through the emotions of misunderstanding, rejection and personal loss of confidence that comes from hurt, is horrendous. However, if we are prepared to leave the consequences with the Lord, it brings spiritual blessing and one can enter into a new experience of identity with the sufferings of the Saviour.

In Isaiah chapter fifty three, Isaiah foretold that Christ would be 'led as a lamb to the slaughter and as a sheep before her shearers was dumb, He did not open His mouth'. We look back to the fulfilment of that prophecy and know that prior to His crucifixion He was treated like a condemned criminal, yet He did not retaliate: then on the cross He died a horrific death between two criminals. He bore it all for the sins of the world and cried 'It is finished'. We know He could have called ten thousand angels to destroy the world and set Him free, but He did not, because our eternal salvation was at stake.

How do we cope with hurt? If we react like the Saviour we will take it and although it is difficult we will pray for grace to accept and reap the benefits of inner peace and the opportunity to identify with His suffering. We are told to rejoice when we are despised. When we do this it is the other party who has to bear the guilt and eventually face his Maker.

Dying to Live

Teach me when I hurt O Lord,
To bear the wound for Thee,
Lift me high above it
Till with my heart I see
This is no painful process
That I must be forced through,
But rather it's a crucible
Where I am made anew

As flames of love enfold me
And refine me as I rest,
Forging deep within me
The bond of perfectness
That binds me to my Saviour
Till wounds cause me no pain,
Since self has died - what triumph!
And Jesus reigns - what gain!

Heather Small

God's Open Hand

READING   Psalm 145

You open your hand and satisfy every living thing.   Psalm 145: 16

*G*od's generosity is characterised by His open hand. Think of it..the God who holds the nations in His hand, the God who created the universe, the God who sent His Son to be the Saviour of the world, opens His hand to you!

We just have to look at the birds. Nature provides for them in winter as well as in summer. I often look at the cotoneaster covered with red berries. How pleasant on a cold winter day to watch the birds peck at these. Sometimes a berry will fall to the ground and the little bird sees it and sweeps down to continue feeding. Birds enjoy God's bountiful provisions. He opens His hand to feed them.

The story is told of a little Scottish lady who was housebound in the Highlands because of a severe winter. She had no food and there was no way for her to get help. She prayed audibly and two lads were outside her cottage laughing at the old lady praying for food. They decided to go to the local shop, buy a loaf, leave it at her door, knock and run away. The lady went to the door and returned praising God for His provision! Someone commented that it was unimportant how the prayer was answered. God had provided for His child!

Hard times may come but God will provide for His children. Those unexpected gifts, the ability to think of better ways to earn money or the wisdom to be more economical - all these are God's generosity and the opening of His hand to provide for us. God's provision is satisfactory. It may not be luxurious but He satisfies every living creature.

In the poverty of communist Russia peasants had to search through the dumps with birds of prey for food. One Christian man found a crust of bread. He cut off the mildew and put it into his bag to bring home. But what satisfaction there was on his face because of his find. He gave thanks to God for opening His hand and providing for him. (Perhaps we should be thinking more about those who are in need and opening our hands to our brothers.)

Besides the provision for our needs God shows us kindness in the changing seasons, in giving us the gift of life, in giving us comfort in sorrow and, above all, in giving us the gift of salvation.

His Faithfulness

He has shown kindness
by giving us rain;
Through changeless seasons
He's always the same;
Summer and Winter,
Autumn and Spring -
let the whole earth
with God's praises ring.

The giver of life,
our comfort in pain,
through days of sorrow -
in death there is gain!
'The grave could not keep Him',
we joyfully sing!
O'er death He was Victor,
so for us there's no sting,

With all creation,
we join in the strain
to Christ our Redeemer,
with whom we shall reign -
to Him who has saved us,
our Lord and our King,
we worship, adore Him -
our homage we bring.

Reaching Out to Others

READING   Psalm 41

'Blessed is he who considers the poor:
The Lord will deliver him in time of trouble.'   *Psalm 41: 1*

*D*avid is not just thinking of the financially poor, but of those who have struggles with health, depression, criticism and all kinds of unpleasant situations. He had experienced difficult circumstances and was grateful for friendship in his hour of need. When he sinned, he felt he had been totally forsaken by everyone, including his close friend -
'Even my own familiar friend in whom I trusted.
Who ate my bread,
Has lifted up his heel against me.' Psalm 41: 9
David feels he is alone in his trouble, but then he realizes that the Lord does not forsake him.
Have we failed to be there for someone who has been wounded by some circumstance in life and feels there is no way forward?
All around us there are hurting people who need a helping hand, and often we are too busy, or too concerned with our own problems, to be able to lend a helping hand to someone in need.
Amy Carmichael was born in Belfast in the later part of the nineteenth century. She had a remarkable experience of God that changed her life and fired her to stretch out a helping hand to others in need.
She had been a Christian for just a couple of years, but as a teenager was not particularly committed to the Lord. One day she was walking home from church with her family and they overtook a little old lady dressed in rags. Amy had never seen such poverty in Presbyterian Belfast. She was moved by the sight and, together with her brothers, she took the woman's arm and helped her along the street. As other church-goers passed by she felt humiliated and resented their proud looks. She felt her face was crimson red as she tried to hide her embarrassment - she said she hated doing it and felt 'crimson all over - soul and body!' But she and her brother plodded on. There was a wet wind blowing about them, and blowing the wet rags of the old woman, till she seemed like a bundle of feathers, and they were unhappily mixed up in them. Just as they passed a fountain, God spoke to her...
'gold, silver, precious stones, wood, hay, stubble, every man's work shall be made manifest, for the day shall declare it, because it shall be revealed by fire and the fire shall try every man's work of what sort it is.'
'If any man's work abide...' 1 Corinthians 3: 12-14a.
These words came to her so clearly that she actually turned to see the voice that spoke! The fountain they had just passed was there, the muddy street had not

changed, the well-dressed church goers, with their quizzical looks was all Amy saw. She said nothing to her brother, but she knew that something had happened that had changed her life's values. Nothing could ever be the same! God had spoken! He rebuked her, challenged her, and she had to take note! After dinner she went to her room and, full of guilt, because of her pride, confessed her sin to the Lord and asked for forgiveness.

The following year, at the age of nineteen, she attended a convention in Glasgow and, for the first time, heard one of the Keswick Convention speakers speak of 'the life of victory'. Amy's heart warmed to the message and she embraced it wholeheartedly and surrendered her life fully to the claims of Christ. She described what happened by likening it to 'her soul in a fog, longing to know how to live a holy life and how to serve her Lord'. As the preacher closed the meeting in prayer, he used the words of Jude 24...

'Oh Lord, we know Thou art able to keep us from falling...!'

Those words fired Amy - she clasped them like someone drowning, took God at His word and rose to go into the future to trust Him, to keep her from falling.

The young Belfast girl was soon to learn that in order for God to 'keep her from falling' she had to learn to be sensitive to the leading of the Holy Spirit. Amy became a true disciple of the Lord Jesus Christ and followed His leading - first to Japan, then to South India, where she founded the Dohnavur Fellowship and stretched out the hand of love and friendship to the children of India.

Did God fulfil His promises to Amy Wilson Carmichael? Yes, He preserved her, He blessed her - the influence of her life will go on into eternity through the children she led to Christ in India. He delivered her on many occasions. He strengthened her on her bed of illness, and although at the last she was confined to bed permanently, through ill health, God used her writing skills to bring blessing to all who read her books. She always requested that a fountain pen be left, filled with ink, on her bedside table. Amy used her pen as an illustration of how God can use a yielded life - the pen had to be clean, it had to be filled and it had to be ready for her to use. In the same way, Amy felt God could take our lives, if they were cleansed and filled with the Holy Spirit, and use them to His glory! May God enable us to obey such instructions, which are totally Bible-based!

Amy Wilson Carmichael remains one of Ulster's most influential Christian poets and writers. Among her lasting contributions to Christian literature, are 'Things as They Are', 'Meal in a Barrel', 'Gold Chord', 'If', 'Edges of His Ways', 'Though the Mountains Shake' , 'Rose from Brier', 'Gold by Moonlight', 'Towards Jerusalem', 'Wings', and 'Figures of the True'. What a legacy!

Values

If I should rise in man's esteem
and only live for self:
My living will have been in vain -
It's as I give, I gain!

If I would make the Lord my choice
and serve Him all my days :
My life will be in service free -
A bright reality!

The Glory of the Rising Sun

READING   Numbers 21: 1-11

'The children of Israel moved on...
and they journeyed... toward the sunrise.'   *Numbers 21: 10,11.*

*L*ed by Moses, the Children of Israel journeyed from Mount Hor to the land of Edom - behind them Egypt and the escape from Pharaoh: before them God's promises of blessing and ample supply of all their needs. How quickly they had forgotten the deliverance from Pharaoh and the guidance and provision of the journey. Instead of being thankful for progress and protection they murmured and complained against God and Moses. God punished their sin and sent fiery serpents whose bite was fatal. As the smell of death filled the air, they cried to Moses and asked him to pray to God for them. The answer did not come as they expected. No doubt they wanted God to remove the serpents so that they could move forward! But God told Moses to make a fiery serpent of brass and put it on a pole for the people to look on and live.

In John chapter three Jesus used this incident in his discourse with Nicodemus - As Moses lifted up the serpent in the wilderness, even so must the Son of Man be lifted up, that whoever believes in Him, should not perish but have everlasting life'.

Before the Children of Israel could travel towards the rising sun their sin had to be dealt with. Before a sinner can travel towards heaven, sin has to be dealt with, and before a redeemed sinner can make progress in the Christian life, sin has to be dealt with. There must be forgiveness by looking to 'the Lamb of God who takes away the sin of the world' and healing through faith in His atoning and redemptive death on the Cross.

There is hope for everyone! We can rise from the ashes of despair to the glory of the rising sun!

Behold the Lamb of God

I gaze upon the dying form
  of Christ the Lamb of God:
    then bow my head and humbly say -
      How could You love me so?
Your bleeding hands and feet and side -
  Such agony I see!
    I don't deserve the price You paid
      to set the sinner free!

I gaze into the empty tomb
  of Christ the Lamb of God:
    then lift my heart and praising, say -
      Your death has ransomed me!
You paid the price for all my sin,
  then rose triumphantly!
    Although I don't deserve Your love -
      Praise God, You rose for me!

God's Righteous Covering

READING   Isaiah 61

'... He has clothed me with the garments of salvation,
He has covered me with the robe of righteousness.'   *Isaiah 61: 10*

*T*he story of Ruth and Boaz is one of the most beautiful love stories ever written. No doubt we are familiar with the story of how Naomi and Ruth returned from the land of Moab, and the events that led up to Ruth gleaning in the field of Boaz. Boaz knew that Ruth was a virtuous woman and, when he finds himself alone with her at night, he gives his garment as a covering for her. This is symbolic of what Christ, our Boaz, did when He died on the cross. He provided a covering to hide us from the wrath of God and the garment of righteousness to prepare us for His Father's presence.

Who has not watched in awe as dignitaries have paraded in their regal attire! Whether it is a band in a uniform, a military display, heads of our country or a celebration in national costume, it is impressive and brings feelings of admiration. What a celebration when the Son of God presents us faultless before His Father, and we stand clothed with the garments of His Son's salvation, and covered with the robe of His righteousness. Let us possess our possessions and stand 'complete in Him'.

Consecration   by Heather Small

'Lord search my heart
In every part,
And as Thy light would shine,
Replace the rags of my
    righteousness
With garments, Lord, of Thine.

That take of me
Which Thou dost see,
That which I cannot discern,
That separates me from
        Thyself,
From all I yet must learn.

Show me that thing
Which does not bring
Honour to Thy Name,
Make the desire of my heart
As Thine own, the same.

Take Thou my heart,
Take every part,
No longer I refuse
The filling of my emptiness
With all that Thou dost choose'.

A Hymn of Praise

READING   Isaiah 12

Therefore with joy you will draw water from the wells of salvation.   *Isaiah 12: 3*

*O*ne might imagine that this delightful little poem should be included in the book of Psalms. But it seems to spring up like an oasis in the desert in the book of Isaiah! It is followed by themes such as 'Mercy on Jacob', 'the Fall of Lucifer' and 'Babylon Destroyed'. Such is the mercy of God in dealing with the fallen race that he mixes blessing with punishment. The scriptures point out sin and unrighteousness and lead us to the grace and forgiveness of God.

Join me today in focusing on God's 'wells of salvation'. It will lift you from grovelling in the 'mire of despair' and take you on wings of praise to the God of our salvation. Draw from the well of peace as you remind yourself that 'great peace have they that love Thy law and nothing shall offend them'. That intended hurt to your spirit will take wings and soar to realms of peace and tranquillity. Draw from the well of love and suddenly you will be released from thoughts of bitterness towards your enemy. Draw from the well of joy and you will rise with a hymn of praise to the Lord. Draw from the well of longsuffering and you will rise with patience to care for the unlovely. Simply 'walk in the spirit' and enjoy the results.

The Third Person of the Trinity

Holy Spirit, Paraclete,
Meet me at the 'mercy seat'
Cleanse me from the guilt of sin,
Nothing in my hand I bring.

Gentle Spirit, heavenly Dove,
Coming on us from above!
Lift my heart on wings of praise.
Unto God an anthem raise!

Mighty Spirit, purging Flame,
I would call upon Your Name:
Burn up all my base desire,
Let me feel the sacred fire.

Does God Still Answer Prayer?

READING   Acts 12: 1-19

'Peter was therefore kept in prison, but constant
prayer was offered to God for him by the church.'   Acts 12: 5

𝒯he result of earnest, believing prayer brought the release of Peter. There was no human intervention either by the prisoners or by the soldiers who were on duty that night in the prison - it was God acting in answer to the corporate prayer by the church. Herod had already put James to death with the sword and, because it pleased the Jews, he decided to imprison Peter and hand him over to be guarded by four squads of four soldiers each. The plan was to bring him out for public trial after the Passover. The night before the trial God intervened. Peter was sleeping between two soldiers, bound with two chains, and sentries stood guard at the entrance. 'Suddenly an angel of the Lord appeared and light shone in the cell. He struck Peter on the side and woke him up'. The chains fell off Peter's wrists and the angel said to him, "Put on your clothes and sandals. Wrap your cloak around you and follow me.' Peter followed the angel out of the prison, passed the guards, and when they came to the iron gate, it opened automatically! The angel accompanied Peter to the end of the street and left him. Peter was stunned and, when he eventually realised what had happened, he went to the house of Mary, John Mark's mother, where Christians were praying.

Does it happen today? Yes many of us have experienced answers to prayer in response to the prayers of others. When John S. Pilbury was Governor of Minnesota the state experienced a plague of grasshoppers that devastated all the crops and the harvest was a complete failure. It ruined some families in the state. the following year a similar plague threatened Minnesota again. What could they do? A number of influential men from various states met in consultation to discuss the situation. A Governor of a neighbouring state urged that the only thing to be done to escape the plague was to call for a day of prayer and ask all people to unite in praying that God would remove the grasshoppers. John S. Pilbury accepted the suggestion, returned home to St. Paul's and issued a proclamation that all people who believed in a God who answered prayer should proceed on a given day to their place of worship and pray to God to remove the grasshoppers from Minnesota. On the appointed day a wonderful thing happened! In some places the grasshoppers died by millions in the trenches; those that were able to fly rose up and flew out of the State of

Minnesota. A few lingered on, but they eventually disappeared, and the crops were saved. There has never been a grasshopper plague in Minnesota since, though there were plagues in other states.

(Dr R A Torrey records this amazing story- He knew John S Pilbury intimately and was a personal friend).

All things are possible!

The only thing beyond the reach
of those who walk with God -
is unbelief that what they ask
may never find reward.
If God has made His purpose clear,
and we know we're in His will,
it's satan brings the doubts, the fears
That God will not fulfil -
So challenge him with Holy Writ;
Remind him God declares...
That what we ask in faith, we have
- God hears, **God answers prayer!**

In His Time

READING   Ecclesiastes 3: 1-11

'He has made everything beautiful in its time.'   *Ecclesiastes 3: 11*

*I*s it not true that when God does not fit into our time schedule we leave Him out of the equation? I am afraid we are all guilty of the 'I'll do it my way' syndrome! However in the Biblical setting of olive oil and wine production, which has an effective but slow process in rural Israel, 'the wheels of God grind slowly'. The rapid changes of the past century have led to the majority concluding that God is too slow for the progress of the twenty-first century. This is far from the truth, because God will work His purposes out in His time and, if we try to stop Him, we will suffer the aftermath of having to reap the consequences of our mistakes.

If we look back in history and consider the time span for artists who have produced major works of art, or if we study the two major wars, success was not accomplished with one splash of paint or one attack of the enemy - it took time and patience! It is recorded of Ford Madox Brown, a sympathizer of the pre-Raphaelite group of artists, that he spent four weeks painting the ribbons on the female's bonnet when painting his most famous painting, 'The Last England'. We have only to consider the long-drawn out war of the twenty-first century in Afghanistan, to conclude that President Bush was right when he declared that the war would take a long time. There is great wisdom in the book of Ecclesiastes - 'To everything there is a season, and a time to every purpose under heaven' (chapter 3: 2).

Chapter three goes on to list some of the time factors in the human life-span. One of the most thought-provoking is 'a time to be born and a time to die'. 'The birth of a child is a time of joy for the whole family. A mother has carried a life for approximately nine months and the time comes for him to be born. Family and friends gather round and admire the little bundle snugly sleeping in his mother's arms. The death of a loved one is a time of great loss and grief but for the one who dies in Christ it is something that can be beautiful. It can be a happy release especially if the dear one has suffered discomfort and pain. John Wesley succinctly said, *'our people die well'*.

A Distant Horizon

I see on yon horizon,
God's final resting place;
I forward press towards it,
Redeemed by sovereign Grace;
My Saviour goes before me,
His Spirit leads the way;
Although my steps may falter,
He is my strength each day.

I see on yon horizon,
People from every race;
They're happy with the Saviour,
And gaze upon His face:
On earth they sought His mercy;
They found in Him their stay;
Life's rugged path's behind them,
In Christ they found the way.

The Redemptive Work of Christ

READING   John 19: 25-37

'They shall look on Him, whom they pierced'.   *John 19: 37*

*W*hen we remember that Christ 'could have called ten thousand angels to destroy the world and set Him free', but 'He did not open His mouth' - He willingly took our punishment because 'without the shedding of blood there is no remission of sin', Christ's redemptive work has a multitude of facets. It is like a precious stone, more valuable and more dazzling than a diamond - it shimmers like crystal and beams hope to a world filled with hatred. One of its sparkling facets is love. Like the lighter gleam of a diamond, love glistens from the risen Saviour to a fallen world. The shaded side of the diamond reflects the scars of the Son of God who gave His back to those who smote Him, His hands and feet to the Roman soldiers who nailed Him to a cross and allowed a sword to be pierced into His side. All facets of the diamond add to its value. Is it any wonder the Cross has drawn multitudes of men and women to accept Salvation as a free gift of God's grace?

John gives us one of the lighter facets of Christ's redemptive work when he wrote, 'God sent not His Son into the world to condemn the world but to save the world through Him', and in the same chapter, John shows a darker facet... 'but whoever does not believe stands condemned already because he has not believed in the name of God's one and only Son'. In chapter six and verse thirty-seven, John highlights the sparkle of the diamond - 'All the Father gives Me shall come to Me, and whoever comes to Me, I will never drive away'. Then the writer to the Hebrews tilts the same gem to remind us of the danger of neglecting God's salvation - 'How shall we escape if we ignore such a great salvation?'

God offers to the whole of mankind, a precious gift, 'without money and without price'. It is available to-day to those who take it. If you have already taken God's gift, pause and thank Him for so great a salvation!

Golgotha

I stood beside Golgotha and heard my Saviour say
'I took your sins upon me - the price I had to pay
Although the path was lonely, there was no other way
For sinful man to enter God's Eternal Day.

I stood beside Golgotha and heard my Saviour pray,
As in His darkest hour, God turned His face away:
What sorrow and what anguish - We never could repay
the debt we owe to Jesus - The Truth: The Life: The Way!

A Shelter in the Storm

'God is our refuge and strength, a very present help in trouble.'   *Psalm 46:1*

One night I was travelling from Co. Fermanagh to Co. Armagh when I was caught in a terrible storm. Flashes of lightning lit up the sky: overhead peals of thunder were deafening: the wind howled and the rain bounced and sparkled on the road ahead. Despite my wind-screen wipers working at the fastest speed, visibility was nil. Between Augher and Aughnacloy it was impossible to drive. On such a lonely stretch of road I did not like the idea of stopping late at night - then, as the lightning lit up the night sky, I saw clearly a neat little cottage on the left some fifty yards from the main road. I turned into the driveway as a blast of thunder roared overhead, hoping the occupants would give me shelter until the storm had passed. On knocking the door a kind gentleman invited me in and he and his wife made me feel welcome. I enjoyed the warmth of their comfortable country kitchen. Their house became my shelter for the next forty minutes. Now every time I pass that house I am reminded of the kind family who gave me shelter from the storm.

On the journey through life we encounter storms. As the strong gales of adversity beat on the frail bark of our lives we feel we will not reach the harbour. Then God comes to our rescue and whispers His peace. Like the hen gathering her chickens under her wings in a storm, God covers us and protects us from danger. I heard a lovely children's story of a grassland that caught fire and spread within a short distance of a small farm. Fortunately, the fire was stopped before it reached the actual farm but much of the surrounding area was totally burned. When the farmer went to inspect the damage he found a group of frightened, motherless chickens. The hen had gathered her chickens under her wings and would not abandon them even though she was burned to death.

Have you the pressure of a family problem? Perhaps you fear the future because of a terminal illness. Exam results are looming ahead and you feel you will not have the grades to get you into your chosen course at university. God wants to be your refuge and strength. He has a plan for you and will bring you through.

Recognize Him today as your refuge and take shelter.

Shelter

How wonderful to know that I
May shelter in the Lord Most High
And as I seek to do His will
May feel His presence, calm and still.

No terror shall possess my life
Although the days are filled with strife,
For he has said, 'My peace is thine
And in the darkness you must shine.'

Dark days, dark nights, but yet my God
Has sent His light into the world
And I, who trust Him, need not fear
The battle which is often near.

(from the collection of poems 'Beauty for Ashes'
by Ruth Wilson, now Mrs Ruth Fullerton)

Restoration

'If you return, then I will bring you back...'   *Jeremiah 15: 19*

How precious these words would sound in the ears of someone who is gravely ill. They would be music to the ear. Equally they should be music to the ear of someone who has gone away from the Saviour and lost his first love. Someone reading this may feel in such a condition - if so, the message of Jeremiah is one of restoration for the cold of heart. To those who feel God has forsaken them, do not give up for God is merciful and will pardon. If God were to judge us we would all be guilty but, thank God, He reminds us that 'there is forgiveness with Him, that He might be feared.' However restoration must be preceded by repentance! - Repentance was the only way back. Jeremiah was struggling with his own sin in this chapter - God was preparing him to be His minister to a rebellious people and before he could call them to repentance, Jeremiah had to meet with God personally. It was a painful experience for Jeremiah - He experienced the loneliness and isolation of God dealing with his soul - He says, 'I was not in the assembly of those who make merry, nor did I rejoice: I sat alone, because Your powerful hand was upon me...' It is a lonely experience and a painful one when God begins to deal with the individual, but it is a marvellous experience and the outcome is blessing. God reminds Jeremiah of His promise - 'I will restore...' (verse 19.) The great man of God comes down to rock bottom - now we can identify with him and sense a fellow-feeling of reality. Jeremiah the prophet, the messenger from God to the people of Israel receives a message to repent!

Have you ever tried to do what Jeremiah did - argue with God, outline your good points? After all Lord, I am a good person at heart: I have never committed murder: I have never done anyone any harm: I am respected in society: I have a good influence on my family: I don't go to the places that sinful men frequent. How like Jeremiah we are! We make excuses but the Lord just gives us the same message - 'Repent.' The dialogue does not stop, for God renewed His promises to Jeremiah, 'I will make you a wall to this people... for I am with you...' How gracious is the Lord! Despite our doubts, the Divine Physician comes to restore. When we repent and turn to Him He always extends to us the hand of mercy. Do not delay but tell God your sin and ask His forgiveness.

1 John 1: 9 'If we confess our sin, He is faithful and just to forgive us our sin and to cleanse us from all unrighteousness.'

Restoration

Restore me the joy of salvation,
touch chords that are lifeless and dead:
Bring peace to my heart; clear my conscience:
Create hunger for life-giving bread!
Give me courage to go and tell others
the message of Your saving grace
that sinners to You be converted -
start running the heavenly race!

Your word gives me cause for rejoicing:
Plainly I read of Your care -
Married You are to the back-slider -
You long for the penitent's prayer!
I take now Your promised forgiveness,
Accept the fresh cleansing You give:
Then out to a world that is dying -
The message of truth I will live!

Panting for God

READING   Psalm 42

'As the deer pants for the water brooks,
so pants my soul for You, O God'.   Psalm 42: 1

*B*ecause of the demands on our time, we find quietness eludes us and we are caught up in a hive of activity from morning til night. There is the train to catch to commute to work: the patter of little feet early in the morning across the bedroom floor awakening you out of a deep sleep: you have not been able to sleep and before dawn you dose off and oversleep: your mind races and the jobs of the day flood your mind so that before even getting out of bed you have started the day's work. Such is the pace of life in the twenty-first century. We have to face the reality of all the demands, and determine to note as a priority, our quiet time on a daily basis - it is difficult and takes a lot of planning and commitment to ensure that our souls are not bereft of nourishment and spiritual refreshment. Just as food and fresh air is essential to healthy living, so time alone with God is necessary for spiritual growth.

Saint Augustine said, 'God made us for Himself and our hearts are restless until they find rest in God.' This is true in the light of God's demand for the sinner's repentance and faith, initially for salvation, but it is also true on a daily basis - a day without time alone with God can be a day of frustration, and ultimately, a day when we do not reach our full potential in the work-place. Certainly a day without time alone with God is a day of spiritual defeat. Find a time that is most suitable to you. The morning is the best time. We are fresh after the rest of the night and our minds (at least for most people) are more alert in the morning. This may not be suitable for you, but work out a suitable time and make sure you profit from it. There are helpful Bible reading notes available in Christian bookshops or you could start with the New Testament and read through the Bible systematically. If you do not understand something, note it down and either look it up in a commentary or ask someone who may be able to help you. The Bible is the inspired Word of God and should be your 'daily bread.' If you do not know how to pray, just start by thanking God for His goodness to you and then tell Him about your difficulties and needs and, before you know, you will have started to pray. Learn to talk to God the way you would talk to your best friend and prayer will become a delight, not a chore. As you progress God will create a hunger for more and you will start to mature and grow spiritually.

'Only God can fully satisfy the hungry heart of man.' *Hugh Black.*

Near to the Heart of God

I stole away to a quiet spot -
Away from the noise of the throng
For deep in my soul was a longing to be
Near to the heart of God.
I whispered a prayer for solitude
And secretly fenced my thoughts
Till the dews of quietness dropped on my soul -
It was the very 'Heart of God!'

I breathed in the freshness of His love
- it was air to my panting soul:
I knew I had found a resting-place
- near to the 'Heart of God.'

The Blessing of Good Parents

READING   2 Timothy 1: 1-14

'Honour your father and your mother that your days may be
long upon the land which the Lord your God is giving you.   *Exodus 20: 12*

*S*ome people find it difficult to express their appreciation to their parents. It's almost as if it's taken for granted that they look after you and care for you without reward, or without knowing it's appreciated. My father gave us instructions about funeral flowers. "No flowers please - flowers should be given while the person is alive and can appreciate them," was his philosophy and that was respected when he died. Whether we express our gratitude with flowers or in words it is something parents would never ask for, or expect, but when it comes spontaneously from a child it brings tremendous satisfaction.

A friend showed me with pride how her son expressed his thanks -
'Dad... Dad, throughout my life you have supported and encouraged me in everything I have done. You've been enthusiastic about my successes and consoled me when things haven't gone well. You've always been patient and kind to me when I've been difficult or down. I really appreciate all the guidance you have given me and I am so proud you are my Dad.
Mum... Mum, you've always been an inspiration to me. You've always been there for me, supporting and encouraging me through all the ups and downs of life, believing in me and making me feel special. I know there are times when I forget to say thanks, but I want you to know how proud and grateful I am to have such a wonderful person to call my mum!'

I am sure you will agree that these are wonderful tributes to good parents. If your parents are still alive and you have never expressed your appreciation to them perhaps it is time to do something about it and let them know that their sacrifice has meant a great deal to you. Parents shape our lives and reproduce themselves through us. To have had good parents is a blessing beyond words - their influence will live for ever. An early American writer summed up the power of influence in the following words... 'When God drops a blessing into the yielded human heart the influences of it are unlimited, its waves are reproduced until they break at last on the shores of eternity.' Thank God for the godly influences on our lives that produce fruit for eternity.

Thank you

Mother, I thank you for just being you!
I know that your love is steadfast and true:
You are frank, you are honest - your motto's not new
- 'Do unto others
What you would like done to you!'

God's Tomorrow

READING   2 Kings 7: 1-2 and Hebrews 11

'... Hear the Word of the Lord.
Tomorrow about this time a measure of fine flour shall be sold
for a shekel, and two measures of barley for a shekel...'   2 Kings 7: 1

*T*he people of Samaria were suffering from a severe famine when suddenly Elisha appeared and said... 'by this time tomorrow... four gallons of barley will be sold in the markets of Samaria for the equivalent of forty pence!' One of the officers, on whom the king was leaning, said, 'That couldn't be even the Lord opened the floodgates of heaven... but you will not eat it.' (2 Kings 7: 2) He didn't, for when God performed the miracle he was trampled to death at the gate. There are lessons to be learned from this account of God's provision for the people of Samaria. The first is that God responds to faith when it is for His glory.

I remember a situation in Argentina. It was All Saints' Day - (Day of the Dead it is called in the north of Argentina) and as it was the custom we all went to the little cemetery - the church members were to bring the light of life to those distraught over loved ones who had died (their only hope was that burning candles at the grave would in some way help them). The provence of Formosa was suffering the worst drought in living memory according to the farmers. Returning from the cemetery I met a farmer who was sceptical about religion and did not have time for any church. 'They have been praying for rain for weeks in the Roman Catholic church,' he commented. 'We have been praying too in the Evangelical Church,' I replied. 'But your God hasn't answered,' he critically said with a shrug of his shoulders. Before I could even think of a reply I said, 'I believe God will answer prayer and send rain before Thursday!' With his 'wait and see' attitude piercing my heart I left my friend. That was Monday and for the next few days I reasoned with God, telling Him His glory was at stake and to please honour His name in this situation so that this sceptical man would realise that God was real and that He did answer prayer. When I saw a little cloud gather I prayed more! Did God fail? The rain came after a six month drought! I did not see the man but I was content knowing that God had answered prayer!

His Faithfulness

He has shown kindness,
By giving us rain:
Through changeless seasons,
He's always the same;
Summer and Winter,
Autumn and Spring:
Let the whole earth
With God's praises ring.

The giver of life,
Our comfort in pain,
Through days of sorrow;
In death there is gain!
'The grave could not keep Him'
We joyfully sing!
O'er death He was victor,
So, for us there's no sting.

With all creation,
We join in the strain
To Christ our Redeemer,
With whom we shall reign,
To Him who has saved us,
Our Lord and our King,
We worship, adore Him -
Our homage we bring.

Opening the Scriptures

READING   Luke 24

'Did not our heart burn within us while he talked with us
on the road and while he opened the scriptures to us.'   *Luke 24 : 32*

*J*ust as all roads lead to the capital of any country, so all roads lead to Jesus Christ in the scriptures. Not every chapter is centred on the Messiah or Christ but all scripture has Jesus Christ as the central key. The aim of all scripture is to reveal God and redeem man.

The secret of understanding the Bible is to know the Author. The Bible does not convey its spiritual truth to the intellectual because it is spirit-breathed. Its writers were borne along by the Holy Spirit when putting down their thoughts. Because of this, it is only the Holy Spirit who can reveal the deep contents of its pages. How wonderful to open the Word of God and find comfort in sorrow: inspiration when under some cloud of doubt: encouragement when grappling with despair: healing for a deep hurt: hope for the future and, above all, assurance for eternity.

God's Word is Precious

God's Word is an island where I love to be -
cut off from the city by road and by sea:
there I bask in sunlight where glorious rays
brighten my pathway along life's rough way.

God's Word is an ocean that I love to sail -
away from a country where evil prevails:
there I breath in freshness that cleanses me through -
I watch for horizons, breathtaking and new.

God's Word is a country that I travel through -
admiring the beauty of landscape so new:
there I behold facets of His majesty -
and thank Him for living - such beauty to see.

Guilty

READING   Isaiah 1: 15-20 and Isaiah 53

'though your sins are like scarlet, they shall be as white as snow,
though they are red like crimson, they shall be as wool.'   *Isaiah 1: 18*

*S*in has been man's problem since our first parents disobeyed in the garden of Eden. It has driven some to despair: it has even driven individuals to suicide. We are reminded daily of its consequences... child abuse, terrorism, robbery of the elderly, and the events of September 11 2001 that changed the world. Sin plagues the conscience with guilt and leads to physical and mental illness. Is there a way of escape? Can I find release from the guilt of my sin? There is only one remedy. It is the forgiveness of God through the atoning death of our Lord Jesus Christ. Pardon for the guilty was purchased at great cost. It took the death of God's Son to bring release from the bondage of sin. He was the just One who took the punishment for the unjust in order to reconcile us to God - What love! 'God so loved the world that He gave His only begotten Son.' Not only did God love but Jesus loved -. 'Greater love has no man than this, that a man lays down His life for His friends'. Jesus willingly gave His life that we might go free.

Guilty

I should have stood in the judgement hall
and answered "guilty" when my name was called,
but God in His mercy, sent His own Son
to take my place, and for my sin atone.

I should have faced the angry throng
for I was guilty and I had done wrong,
but Jesus accepted His father's will
and suffered alone on Golgotha's hill.

I should have been nailed to a cross of shame
for I am part of man's fallen race,
but wonder of wonders, the price has been paid
and the debt of my sin on Jesus was laid

Life After Death

READING   John 11: 1-46

'Jesus said to her, "I am the resurrection and the life;
he who believes in Me, though he may die, he shall live.'   *John 11: 25*

Rachel phoned me yesterday - it was the anniversary of a tragic accident in her family when her son-in-law was killed and also two of her darling grandchildren. The family had been celebrating a birthday and, returning from a hotel, had a serious accident. I knew the details and Rachel did not have to tell me the grief the whole family had been through. She had kept in touch with prayer requests for some months and I had shared her grief in some little way. God wonderfully answered prayer in restoring her daughter and grandson to a reasonable measure of health, but the pain was still there and the reality of such a loss was something with which she and the others would always have to come to terms. The world moves on and families like these are left with their grief and pain. I had sent Rachel a copy of my first book, 'Daily Gems of Truth' and she just wanted to let me know that she was finding it helpful. That brought comfort to me! Since Rachel's phone call I have been thinking of all the other friends who have had similar experiences and are nursing a grief that others can't share. I think of Joan who not only has had to come to terms with the loss of her daughter Marie in the Enniskillen bomb tragedy, but the loss of a dear son and husband... Joan has also had to deal with the aspect of forgiveness in her grief. After talking to Joan recently I asked myself; 'Have the people who planted the bomb no heart?... Have they no family of their own? Do they not realise the pain they have caused innocent people?'

If you are struggling with grief today and trying to find answers, I do not have the answers, but I want to tell you about my Friend who uderstands your grief... 'What a friend we have in Jesus, all our sins and griefs to bear, What a privilege to carry everything to God in prayer'. Rachel said, 'Vera, what do people do without the Lord in times of sorrow and loss? He has helped us through the past year.' Allow Him to give you His healing balm - See Him weep with Mary and Martha on the death of their brother: listen to His words of comfort, 'I am the resurrection and the life'. There is life alter death - Marie and Emma will never grow old! I cannot enter into the pain, but I want grief-stricken mothers, fathers and family members to know that the Saviour understands your pain and loss and will be with you! Be comforted by His words today and go into the future knowing that 'His grace is sufficient for you for His strength is made perfect in weakness.' He has a plan for the rest of your life and will use you to bring comfort and healing to others.

No answers

Though I don't understand
    the mystery of pain -
I know that in nature
    it takes sunshine and rain
for the earth to produce an abundance of grain.

Though I don't understand
    the mystery of pain -
I know God understands
    and will one day explain
that the dark threads of life were for personal gain.

'Not till the loom is silent and the shuttle cease to fly,
will God unroll the canvas and explain the reason why'.
(Quotable quote)

Lord, Teach Us to Pray

READING   Matthew 6: 1-15

'Our Father, in heaven, hallowed be Your name.'   *Matthew 6: 9*

Is the Lord's Prayer relevant for today? I don't say it every day but when I do, it is special! As a child, saying the Lord's Prayer to me was praying! But at sixteen years of age I discovered the reality of knowing Christ as my Saviour and Lord.   As a new Christian I did not know how to begin to pray. Then I started...'Our Father...' Suddenly, the realisation that something had happened, dawned 'I had been adopted into the family of God! I started the prayer again, but this time I prayed, "**My Father**..." It was the greatest experience of my life. For the first time I was able to call God my Father, and the Lord's Prayer took on a totally new meaning. That was how I began to pray... so for me the Lord's Prayer was very relevant. Before I could even formulate a prayer, I had started to pray. I started by thanking God for bringing me into His family and making me His child. I could hardly believe what was happening - I now had a relationship with my Maker and I was linked to heaven by a mysterious re-birth that enabled me to call God 'Father' for the first time. That has never changed and never will! In fact it has developed into an intimacy with God that I trust will deepen until my earthly race is over and I go to be with Him for ever.

Is there someone reading this today who feels he cannot pray? Begin as I did! Start with the Lord's Prayer. Meditate on the opening two words and then ask yourself - 'Is God MY Father'?' If the answer is no then now is the time to do something about it. Receive Jesus Christ as your personal Saviour.

John 1: 12, reminds us that 'As many as received Him to them He gives the right, the authority to become children of God...'

Take time to Pray

Take time to pray
When the pressures of life
Strip you of poise,
And nothing seems right;
When trivial things
Are mountains so high
They look insurmountable
And friends pass you by.

Take time to pray
While others are bent
On fortune and fame
Their heart is intent:
They don't seem to worry,
Or think of the cost
Of their soul in such danger -
Eternally lost!

Take time to pray,
Even others may mock;
Faith is the key
Bolted doors to unlock;
There's never a problem
That's too hard for Him;
To a wonderful Saviour,
No impossible thing.

Take time to pray
For inward release;
Jesus will help you
And give you His peace:
To the broken in heart
He pours out His balm;
Storm-tossed on the sea of life -
He wants to bring calm.

Take time to pray,
You're part of God's plan
To carry the Gospel
To some distant land:
The world has its heroes,
But reapers are few;
For the cause of the kingdom,
Is He calling you?

Take time to pray
We can treasure lay up
Where moth and rust
Cannot reach and corrupt:
Soon life will be over,
Death's valley we cross;
Will our work stand the fire?
Or will we suffer loss?

Leaning on the Everlasting Arms

READING   Isaiah 43: 1-7 and Deuteronomy 33: 27

'The eternal God is your refuge
and underneath are the everlasting arms.'   *Deuteronomy 33: 27*

*W*hen we face situations that we cannot handle we need someone to see us through. There are times when our family and friends are able to help us and we find a release in sharing our burdens. At other times even they cannot ease our pain. You may be facing the unknown. It could be a change of job, unemployment, loneliness, major surgery, a terminal illness or the valley of the shadow of death. Whatever your difficulty today, God is with you. He will not fail you or forsake you. In fact He reminds you that he is the 'Eternal God.' What a thought - He never had a beginning and will never have an end!   You are the child of His love whom He formed and knows intimately. He knew you before you were formed. He knew you in the womb and He has known the course of your life to this present moment. He will not leave you now!

When I think of 'refuge' I see myself stopping on the six-mile walk at the Giant's Causeway. It is winter. The boisterous waves crash on the rocks and send enormous sprays high into the air, then fall helplessly back and disappear into the angry sea. I look up to where the birds are perched high in the alcoves looking at the turbulent sea with a frightened flutter of their wings. They have found refuge in a secure place. They know the dangers but the waves will not disturb their tranquillity. They are safe. God reminds you today that you are safe in Him for He is your refuge. 'Everlasting arms' underneath you! How reassuring! With those arms underneath you will not sink. Tell Him how insecure you feel, how frightened you are of the future. Throughout the book of Deuteronomy we read of 'arms stretched out' towards Israel. It is reassuring to know that despite their disobedience God was there with His everlasting arms stretched out to them. He is the same now - His arms are stretched out to you today. Cast your burdens on Him and find security in His everlasting arms - just rest in His promise and leave the future in His hands.

Everlasting Arms

Everlasting Arms I need You
Everlasting Arms I feel You
Underneath and round about me
- setting mind and spirit free.

Everlasting Arms enfold me
Everlasting Arms please hold me
In the strength of Your embrace
'till I run my earthly race.

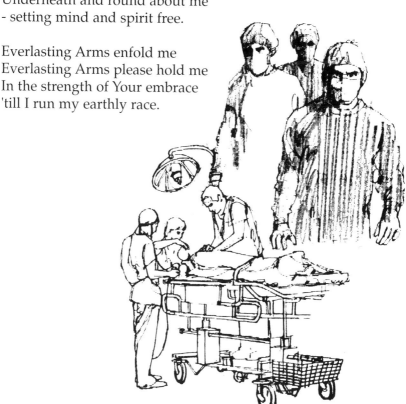

Guidance

'... present your bodies.... that you may prove
what is that good and acceptable and perfect will of God.'   *Romans 12: 1, 2*

*G*uidance is like a jig-saw puzzle in a number of ways. Jig-saws come in different sizes suitable for all ages. A child begins placing simple shapes together to produce a picture. With age it gets more complicated, until adults, who still enjoy the pastime, face challenges of thousands of pieces - much to the annoyance of a wife or family member who finds this a terrible inconvenience in the home. Guidance begins like the simple jig-saw puzzle. God leads us along by guiding us with the milk of the Word, and confirms it through other people and circumstances, until we sense we are moving in the right direction. Then the pieces seem to get more numerous as we take up burdens and responsibilities. We find ourselves with a more complicated network of circumstances and feelings to work through as we come to terms with the principle of weighing up decisions in the light of God's Word.

Four important components in building a jig-saw puzzle are frustration, dilemma, satisfaction and completion. I have found it to be similar over the years regarding guidance. As a teenager I became so frustrated about guidance that I found myself in a dilemma. The future loomed ahead and, as a Christian, I did not want to make a mistake and miss the will of God for my life, so I seriously looked at the options. Yes I had surrendered my life to God as taught by the apostle Paul in Romans chapter twelve but I could not find my way. I sensed God was calling me into His service, but to which Bible College should I apply for training? I wrote to one and the reply came back – I was too young. I was asked if I would come and help on the staff for a time. I sought advice and was wisely told to wait. To where would I go from here? It was a bit like looking at a complicated jig-saw puzzle and feeling frustrated and then attempting to put a couple of pieces together only to find that they did not fit. I was in a dilemma. Then one day I read in Oswald Chambers' book 'So Send I You' – 'the will of God is not a problem to be solved but a revelation to be waited for'. I felt a total release of tension and frustration and suddenly I was at peace, knowing that God would reveal it to me in His time, not mine. When I applied to Emmanuel Bible College I knew I would be accepted for training when I posted my application form because God had guided me. What satisfaction when I sailed across the Irish Sea and commenced my studies. When graduation came there was a sense of completion - I had finished one jig-saw puzzle and was starting another. It has been the same at every stage of my life...

I look back with a tremendous sense of satisfaction and assurance that I have been guided at every stage in my life and now sense that same sense of peace in having obeyed what I believe to be the will of God for my life. Young person, the will of God is 'good, acceptable and perfect'. Do not be afraid of the Lord's prohibitions for He has purposes to bless you and lead you in the pathway of guidance. He has a 'blue-print' for your life - Don't miss it. If you are an older reader, it is not too late to surrender to the Lordship of Jesus Christ and prove what is that good and acceptable will of God' for the rest of your life. It is an exciting and challenging life. Fellowship with your Lord becomes a great adventure. To complete a very complicated jig-saw puzzle brings tremendous satisfaction, but is nothing compared with experiencing, in your walk with God, one jig-saw puzzle after another being completed as you journey through life in the will of God. Remember at the frustrating and dilemma stages there is the satisfaction and joy of completion ahead.

Completion

When my journey through life will have ended;
My feet reached eternity shore:
Oh how glad I shall be that I yielded
to Christ, the great potter of yore:
If the way now seems rough and I wonder
why God in His love sends the storms -
May I cling to my heavenly Lover
- protection to find in His arms.

Trusting in the Shadow of His Wings

READING   Psalm 63

*'Because You have been my help, therefore
in the shadow of Your wings I will rejoice'.*   Psalm 63: 7

*D*avid's opening words in this Psalm reveal his thirst for God. He had obviously known a special encounter with the power and glory of the Lord in the sanctuary and again he longs for what he had experienced and seen. It is often the case that in times of special need God reveals Himself to His children. Those who have gone through deep sorrow have emerged with fresh revelations of the Lord. His promises have become more meaningful and they seem to have gone from one realm of intimacy with God to another. It is difficult to know how one would react if faced with a terminal illness, or if a close member of our family, or a dear friend was diagnosed with cancer. You may have had that experience and known the strength and grace of God in such circumstances. Or you may be faced with such trauma in the future.

On 30th January 2000, Rae noticed a swelling on her son David's neck. She made a doctor's appointment for David for the following Wednesday but on Tuesday night when he returned from a day trip to Dublin he looked ill so was taken to Accident and Emergency in Craigavon Area Hospital. It was later confirmed that David had Hodgkin's Disease, cancer of the lymphatic system. On the day David went for a biopsy of one of the glands, Rae's daily reading was most appropriate - 'Oh God Thou are my God, early will I seek Thee', Psalm 63: 1. The reading continued, with an illustration and read, 'Hear His voice and the doctor's report won't fill you with fear'. On Wednesday morning, 16th February, a doctor telephoned from the hospital asking to speak to David. As David was in Belfast, it was not possible to know the outcome of the biopsy. Rae recalls her reaction - "I went straight to my daily reading and got the heading, 'God can weave the thorns of life into a Crown of Glory'. I just put my head back on the sofa and I sobbed sore to God. I remember saying, 'Lord, three years ago I couldn't part with David to go to University in Scotland but today I am handing him completely over to you. He is Yours. His outcome in life depends solely on you and if you choose to use him he has to come through this'. I remember saying this to David and he said, 'That's right Mum, I am God's'".

As a mother, Rae would have preferred the diagnosis, instead of her son. She shared the pain of chemotherapy and radiotherapy with David. Rae recalls December 11th when David started radiotherapy, which lasted until 9th January -

"He travelled Monday to Friday to Belvoir Hospital, only getting Christmas and New Year's Day off. He had twenty treatments in total. It was during one of these days, as I was waiting for David that I read a poem in a book titled, 'Peace be still', based on Mark 4: 39 and John 14: 37...

'When the storm around you rages
And you're going through the mill,
Remember the words that Jesus said -
In the tempest - 'Peace, be still'.

"Again I had been assured of God's love and presence, and at times when I thought I was on my own He spoke to me through this poem'. In secret, many a tear drop fell but none of which God did not know about, and it was in these times that I gained my inner strength through knowing that people of all ages were upholding our family in prayer. This is something I hold very dear. "Two favourite hymns were 'What a Friend we have in Jesus' and 'Jesus Friend Unfailing'. When trials come our way we do not know the outcome, but one thing I do know is that 'Jesus Friend Unfailing' will provide us with the grace and strength to get through, come what may.

"David's future, like all of our own is in the hands of our Heavenly Father".

Comfort

God has arms strong enough
to lift the universe,
yet gentle as a mother
He will come and ease the stress
of weary pilgrims on the road
to everlasting bliss -
His arms caress, He gives the kiss
of peace to troubled breast!

God's Handiwork

READING   Psalm 8

*'When I consider the works of Thy hand...
what is man that You are mindful of him.'*   Psalm 8: 3a, 4a

*W*ho has not stood spellbound when some panoramic view has come into sight? My most outstanding and breath-taking experience was when touring in the Andes in Argentina. There was one magnificent view after another as we drove to within just under two miles of the highest point, where the engine of the jeep would not function because it was not adjusted for high altitude. We could not make it to the 'Christ of the Andes' statue which marks peace between the two nations but words failed to describe the beauty! "Que majestad! Quo hermosa!" Even in the Spanish language we were lost for words. The descent was equally magnificent. A family from our church in the province of Formosa were my travelling companions and as we descended to fifteen thousand feet above sea level, the railway track from Argentina to Chile was on our right and just beyond it was a fast flowing river. As we watched the river suddenly we reached a point where two rivers meet and unite for a swift descent to the fertile valley below. I decided to bathe my foot in the torrent of water, but, to my dismay, it was so cold I could almost feel my feet freezing - my toes were numb. The only way I could describe it was "defrosted ice water from the freezer." Although the water was freezing, the air was fresh and a little warm. We drank handfuls of the sparkling water: then sat and drank in the beauty of God's handiwork. Above us the great Andes with Aconcagua, the sixth highest peak in the world, towered in splendour and her height and blanket of snow defied an ascent. Below us was the meandering River Negro. Lower down we stopped where the Rio Negro and the Rio Blanco meet and plunge in a relentless descent to the fertile plains of Mondoza. What a sight! The view and atmosphere were almost frightening in their majesty. It is indelibly engraved on my mind and heart.

Since that I have seen so much of God's handiwork. Some of the most memorable are the Niagra Falls, the Rocky Mountains and 'The Sound of Music' area. As you read and rejoice in the beautiful views that fill your horizon, give thanks again to our great God, who has given us richly all things to enjoy. We have marvellous sights here in Ireland and throughout the United Kingdom. Our beautiful Mourne Mountains and the Antrim coast have given us joy on many occasions. We have marvelled at God's spectacular and unique handiwork at the Giant's Causeway. People from all over the world have come to view its magnificence. What a great Creator! It leaves us asking with the Psalmist - 'What is man that Thou art mindful of him?'

A Lake in winter

Silent, motionless, cradled in the arms of nature:
Its waters mirror the moods of a changing sky
reflecting an upturned forest
with sharp pines piercing its depth
to produce an image that would catch an artist's eye:
How splendid the reeds and rushes that frame its meandering
 border!
How elegant the swans that rise with graceful charm!
No sound intrudes the peaceful sleep - for here the soul of man
and nature meet
- acknowledging a work sublime:
No canvas needed!
It's divine!

(Written by a lake in winter on the road from Enniskillen to Sligo 1996)

Searching for Reality

READING   Psalm 42: 1-11

'Why are you cast down, O my soul:
And why are you disquieted within me?'   *Psalm 42: 5*

*T*he eighteenth century produced some of our greatest poets. William Wordsworth is one of the best known of this period, but one of the lesser known is John Clare, who made a valuable contribution to English literature. In his poem 'I AM', he unveils a search for reality within the soul - an emptiness defined by St Augustine as 'a vacuum that only God can fill.' For our meditation today, it would be profitable to look at the poem and place it before the mirror of Scripture, diagnose the problem and apply the God-given remedy.

I Am
by John Clare (1793 - 1864)

I am: yet what I am none cares or knows,
	My friends forsake me like a memory lost;
I am the self-consumer of my woes,
	They rise and vanish in oblivious host,
Like shades in love and death's oblivion lost;
	And yet I am, and live with shadows tost.

Into nothingness of scorn and noise,
	Into the living sea of waking dreams,
Where there is neither sense of life nor joys,
	But the vast shipwreck of my life's esteems;
And e'en the dearest - that I loved the best -
	Are strange - nay, rather stranger than the rest.

I long for scenes where man has never trod;
	A place where woman never smiled or wept;
There to abide with my Creator, GOD,
	And sleep as I in childhood sweetly slept:
Untroubling and untroubled where I lie;
	The grass below - above the vaulted sky.

The first time I read Clare's poem, I felt a strange sadness. Was there nobody in his circle of friends who could help him? If this is an expression of an inner quest for reality, which it seems to be, then why did nobody tell him God's answer to his problem?

If you have a similar vacuum in your soul and sense a hunger for reality, I want to assure you that Christ can fill that vacuum. If you are forsaken by friends, then there is a friend who will be a father, a husband or wife to you - He will stick 'closer than a brother'. Do you feel lost in the shadows of adversity and despair? God offers you solace because He is the way to happiness and will bring you out into the sunlight of His love. 'Cast your burden on the Lord and He will sustain you'.

Are you trying to swim through 'the sea of waking dreams, or wallow in the mire of the nothingness of scorn and noise'? I have good news for you - Jesus Christ is prepared to come into your life by His spirit and 'with Christ in the vessel, you can smile at the storm as you go sailing home!' You may be going through the heartache of bereavement or the loss of a true friend - perhaps you feel let down by someone you trusted and you are afraid to trust anyone now. My dear friend, Jesus wants to help you! Talk to someone. Don't bottle it up inside any longer. Be assured that 'the Saviour can solve every problem, the tangles of life He can undo; there's nothing too hard for Jesus, there's nothing that He cannot do.' Don't be like the one described in Clare's poem and dream of a distant future when relief will come. Turn to the Saviour now and find in Him your solace and joy. It really does work! Trust Him!

Seeking for Happiness

I sought for lasting happiness
    to fill my empty soul
and satisfy my longing
    to be completely whole:
Deep within I knew the pain
    of doubt and guilt and fear
but sadly in a busy world
    no one seemed to care,
or sense a fellow-feeling
    of a vacuum deep inside
which I longed to share with someone
    in whom I could confide:

Then Jesus drew me to Him
    and wiped the falling tear
He poured in the balm of healing
    and took away my fear:
He pardoned my transgressions;
    He wiped the slate so clean
that guilt and doubt just left me
    and my soul felt whole and clean:
now I can share with others
    His joy and peace and love
and tell them -LASTING HAPPINESS
    COMES ONLY FROM ABOVE!

Mustard Seed Faith

READING   Matthew 17: 14-23

'If you have faith like a grain of mustard seed, you will say to this mountain,
"Be removed and carried into the sea," and it shall be done.'   *Matthew 17: 20a*

*T*he first time that George Inglis went to America he crossed the Atlantic with, in his words, 'One of the most devoted men he ever met'. Off the coast of Newfoundland the captain told George Inglis the following remarkable story.

"Mr Inglis the first time I crossed here, five weeks ago, one of the most extraordinary things happened that has completely transformed my life. Up to that time I was an ordinary Christian. We had a man of God on board, George Muller of Bristol. I had been on the bridge for twenty-two hours and never left it. Someone tapped me on the shoulder - I was startled! It was George Muller.
'Captain,' he said, 'I have come to tell you that I must be in Quebec on Saturday afternoon.' This was Wednesday. 'It is impossible,' I said. 'Very well, if your ship can't take me God will find other means to take me. I have never broken an engagement in fifty years.' 'I would willingly help you. How can I? I am helpless.' 'Let us go down to the chart room and pray.' I looked at the man of God and I thought to myself – 'What lunatic asylum could the man have come from?' I never heard of such a thing. 'Mr. Muller,' I said, 'Do you know how dense the fog is?' 'No,' he replied, 'My eyes are not on the density of the fog, but on the living God who controls every circumstance of my life.'
He got down on his knees and prayed a simple prayer. I muttered to myself, 'That would suit a children's class where the children were not more than eight or nine years old!' The burden of his prayer was something like this: 'O Lord, if it is consistent with Thy will please remove this fog in five minutes. Thou knowest the engagement made for me in Quebec for Saturday. I believe it is Thy will.' When he finished I was going to pray but he put his hand on my shoulder and told me not to pray. 'First you do not believe He will, and second, I believe he has, so there is no need for you to pray about it.' I looked at him and George Muller said this: 'Captain, I have known the Lord for fifty seven years and there has never been a single day that I have failed to gain an audience with the King. Get up Captain and open the door and you will find the fog is gone.' I got up and the fog was gone! You tell that to some people of a scientific mind and they will say, 'That is not according to natural laws.' 'The God with whom we have to do is omnipotent. Hold on to God's omnipotence. Ask in faith.' On Saturday afternoon, I may add, George Muller was there on time."

Faith can move Mountains

Faith is a shield for us to use when Satan wages war
Upon the conscience and the mind in your weakest hour:
So take the Spirit's sword in hand
The shield of faith to guard,
Then surely you will conquer -
And gain your 'Promised Land'

Heaven is My Eternal Home

READING   Revelation 22: 1-6

*'And there shall be no more curse: but the throne of God
and of the Lamb shall be in it and His servants shall serve Him.'*   *Revelation 22: 3*

*T*he first six verses of Revelation chapter twenty-two give us one of the most beautiful glimpses of heaven we have in Scripture. Many things we do not know about heaven but we do know that there will be 'a pure river of water of life, clear as crystal, proceeding from the throne of God and of the Lamb.' I love to watch the river in its different moods and I am thrilled that there will be a river in heaven! This river will be different because it will be 'clear as crystal.' The rivers of earth flow down, collecting mud, grit and sand in their irresistible flow to the great oceans of the world - even shallow rivers flowing over pebbles could not be described as 'clear as crystal'. The last river we shall cross on earth will be the river of death. David calls it 'the valley of the shadow of death'. The mud and grit of a sinful world is responsible for the 'shadow', but that will be changed on the other side. How comforting to know that there will be a 'crystal river' beyond the river of death! There will be 'no more curse.'

Sin brought the curse of God on the whole human race, but John reminds us that this will be left behind. Oh the relief to know there will be no more curse in heaven. For the many who fear the darkness and are frightened at night there is good news for you - 'there is no night there'... Dear friend, heaven is a wonderful place! If you have loved ones who have died in Christ they are 'Safe in the arms of Jesus'... and that is the most secure place. John says, 'And they shall see His face: and His name shall be on their foreheads'.

Journey's End

When I am gone
   Sing no sad songs
For sadness to
   This world belongs,
But from your heart
   An anthem raise
Of joyous and
   Triumphant praise.

When I am gone
   Lay no wreaths there
For sun and storm
   to strip and bare,
But sow some seed
   Yours faith to prove,
And let the flowering
   Be of love.

When I am gone
   Grieve not for me,
From cage of clay
   At last set free,
But peel the bells
   With gladsome lay
To speed my spirit
   On its way.

Jean Corbett

Ask and Receive

READING   Luke 11: 1-13

For everyone who asks receives, and he who seeks
finds, and to him who knocks it will be opened.   Luke 11: 10

*S*ometimes God answers a cry from the heart immediately and we have incidents recorded both in Scripture and from the biographies of men and women who, down through the   history of the Christian church, have experienced remarkable deliverance in answer to the prayer of faith. God is able, and does answer the urgent cry from the heart, but sometimes He wants to teach us lessons of patience and endurance, so delays the answer. Amanda Smith, the coloured American evangelist who was greatly used by God throughout the United States of America, writes of a particular time of testing financially. Before leaving to go on a mission to Salem, she needed ten dollars to pay two months rent,and her shoes were worn out - she did not have the money to either pay the rent or buy a new pair of shoes. Her simple faith and explicit account of God's amazing answer to prayer is refreshing to read!

"I told the Lord I was willing to go with the shoes I had, if He wanted me to, but they were broken in the sole". I said, "Lord, Thou knowest if I get my feet wet I will be sick. Now, if it is Thy will to get the shoes, either give me some work to do or put it in the heart of somebody to give me the money to get the shoes." These words came to my heart -'If Thou canst believe, all things are possible to him that believeth.' I said, "Lord, the shoes are mine, and I put them on as really as I ever put on a pair of shoes in my life!" Oh, how real it was! Some three days after, I said to a friend, "I want to go to Seventh Street before I go away, for I promiśed, and I have never had the chance to go". We had a good prayer and testimony meeting. The Lord helped me to speak, and I told them that the Lord was sending me to Salem. At the close, friends gathered round me, and as old Father B. passed out he said, 'Good-bye, Sister Smith'. He shook my hand and put something in it. I thanked him, put it in my pocket, and went home. As I sat by the fire thinking about the meeting, I began to get very drowsy. 'Well', I thought, 'I must get off to bed'. Then the thought came to me - 'You had better see what that money is Father B. gave you.' I took it from my pocket. There was one two-dollar bill and three one-dollar bills. It was the first time I had ever had so much money given to me in my life, just for nothing, like, and I thought I must have made a mistake in counting it, so I counted it again. Yes, it was really five dollars. Just then a voice whispered, 'You know you prayed about your shoes.' 'Oh' I shouted, 'Yes, Lord'. I remember now. Praise the Lord! I was so happy I could hardly go to sleep. It was the Lord's doing, and it was marvellous."

Unbelief

"Isn't this the carpenter?
Isn't he Mary's son?
Aren't his sisters and brothers four
Known to us everyone?

"What is his right to lecture us?
We're just as wise as he.
How dare he preach in our synagogue?
On whose authority?"

So Jesus left His own home town
Amazed and full of grief,
For He could do no miracles there
Because of their unbelief.

And throughout His earthly pilgrimage
And still from heaven's throne
He waits for faith to unlock the door
Of blessing upon His own.

Jean Corbett

The Need to be Still in a Busy World

READING   Psalm 46

'Be still and know that I am God...'   *Psalm 46: 10a*

*T*here are times when we need to be still and recognise that there are certain things that are completely out of our control. Often it is when we take our hands off and let God take control that we see answers to our prayers. This is true in our own personal walk with our God and in His dealing with others. It is especially true in special times of revival when God gives miraculous manifestations of His omnipotent power. If you feel that things are out of control in your life, perhaps God would have you 'take stock'. We have all been guilty of letting the demands of work and other pressures build up and have had to slow down.

Dr. Sangster *wrote two years before his death...*
'Slow me down, Lord, give me amidst the confusion of my days the calmness of the everlasting hills. Break the tension of my nervous muscles with the soothing music of the singing streams that live in my memory! Help me to know the magic restoration power of sleep; teach me the art of taking minute vacations, of lowering down to look at a flower, to chat to a friend, to pat a dog, to read a few lines from a good book. Slow me down, Lord; and inspire me to send down my roots deep into the soil of life's ending values that I may grow towards the stars and my great destiny. Amen'.

What helps you to relax? For some it is reading a good book, for others it is bodily activity such as swimming, jogging, sports, gardening, a particular hobby, time spent with friends, etc. Take time to unwind and enjoy the simple things of life. In our devotions our sense of God depends on our detachment from our daily activities. We must draw near to God before He draws near to us! To experience the renewing of the Holy Spirit in our lives we must submit to the pull of God on our spirits and allow Him to minister to our daily needs.

A Prayer for Tranquillity

Slow me down, Lord!
Give me the tranquillity of a boat
Anchored in a calm harbour!
Slow me down, Lord!
Help me relax, while others pass in the
'rat-race' of this busy life:
Slow Me down, Lord!
'til nestled in the Rock of Ages
I am re-formed by the Creator of the universe;
I am re-filled by the Divine Paraclete;
I am renewed to fresh endeavour
For the Saviour who bought me with His blood
And gave me the privilege of representing Him
In a lost world!
Slow me down, Lord!
Give me the tranquillity of a bird nestled in
The cleft of the rock!
Slow me down, Lord:
Help me relax while others wrestle with the gales
Of an angry sea;
Slow me down, Lord!
'Till, anchored in the Rock of Ages,
- I am reassured by the Captain of my Salvation
- I am reminded of His un-erring plan;
- I have re-assessed lasting values;
Then let me rise with sense of purpose
To sail into the irresistible future
With the stamp of tranquility
Indelibly marked on my passport to eternity.

God Guides us Through His Word

READING   Psalm 119: l05-112

'Your Word is a lamp to my feet and a light to my path.'   *Psalm 119: 105*

Just as knowing Christ as Saviour and Lord is the key to understanding the Bible, so developing a love for the scriptures is the key to spiritual growth and our guide for life. The Bible is different from any other book because it is the 'Living Word' to which we come again and again and see fresh aspects of truth. How often one opens the scriptures and, although the chapter is familiar, somehow, a truth jumps from the pages with fresh understanding and revelation! God's word is relevant to every aspect of our daily life. Life is a preparation for eternity and the word of God gives us clear guidelines and instructions to prepare. It is the wise person who heeds the instructions and follows the Guide. Life is a journey from the cradle to the grave. We need a guide for our journey otherwise we will take the wrong turn and end in disaster. God has given us a guide and whispers - "My Word is a lamp to your feet and a light to your path". It is the wise man who studies the map to find the right course and it is the wise man who turns to the scriptures to find the way.

I recall being caught in a thunderstorm when I worked in Argentina. It was a terrifying experience. I had been visiting all afternoon in a slum area on the outskirts of the city. The homes were just shacks of wood and corrugated tin. Leaving Chacra Venticinco on my scooter and still on the dust road, a sandstorm blew up and I found myself in what must have been 'the eye of the storm'. Blinded by the dust I felt I was suffocating. I cried to the Lord for help and guidance. Coughing and spluttering I pushed my scooter forward with my eyes closed. The thought of death by suffocation crossed my mind but God heard my prayer and, miraculously, I entered a clear area, started the scooter and headed into the city. I left behind that cloud of dust with my heart beating rapidly and a feeling of gratitude to God for His deliverance. When I opened my eyes and looked back I saw the dark cloud of dust. It was a wonderful feeling to be able to breathe again!

The Will of God

In the centre of the circle
Of God's will I rest;
Perfect peace: divine contentment
His unerring plan is best!
Not the way of ease He chooses,
Nor what I thought might be right,
But a better, higher pathway,
pleasing in my Father's sight!

In the centre of the circle
Of God's will I walk:
Oh the joy of sweet communion,
As with Him I often talk!
Here I prove His will is perfect
– good, acceptable to me!
Gone the stress of my own striving
For a plan that I could see!

In the centre of the circle
Of God's will I run
In the race that's set before me,
Guided by 'the unseen One';
He gives patience when it's needed
'Author, Finisher of the faith'!
And when dangers strew
    the race course,
He gives me amazing grace!

In the centre of the circle
Of God's will I see
Heathen in their sin and
    blindness -
I must go by air or sea!
Tell them of the Father's mercy,
Of a Saviour from above,
Of a home prepared by Jesus –
Tell of His redeeming love!

In the centre of the circle,
Of God's will I find
There are joys and there are
    sorrows
From a Father good and kind!
In my sorrows He is with me,
In my joys He shares a part,
Daily He is near to guide me
To the goal and final mark!

God's Way is Perfect

READING   Psalm 18: 23-36

'As for God, His way is perfect, the word of the Lord is proven.
He is a shield to all who trust in Him'.   Psalm 18: 30

When a master potter takes the clay and begins to mould and fashion it, we do not know what he has in mind. His skill is evident as he prepares for firing and glazing, but it is not until the precious vessel is complete that we see the expertise of the craftsman. He knew from the beginning, but we only know when the final process is completed. Similarly, God takes the clay of our lives and in the process of making 'a vessel unto honour and meet for the Master's use' we do not see what He has in mind. We only feel the pain of His hands as he moulds the clay. It is only as we yield to His touch and allow Him to take control that the perfect vessel will emerge. Often it is in the storms of life that God's chisel does its deepest work and a 'new vessel' emerges, as seems fit for the Potter.

David, a young university student, has derived strength from the Psalms - Particularly Psalm 18:30, which is the verse for today, Psalm 62:1-2 and Psalm 121: 1-2.
"On 16th February 2000, I was diagnosed with Hodgkin's Disease, cancer of the lymphatic system. It was six weeks after I had celebrated my 21st birthday and I was in my third and final year at Queen's University. Learning of my diagnosis raised many questions in my mind. What was this disease? How did it ever come to be in my body? Why me? How would I cope with chemotherapy? As a Christian, I was looking for God's plan in all of this. Initially I felt confused, why would a God who loves me let this happen to me?
I was frustrated and perhaps angry that this was happening to me at this particular time. I would come to learn that the future I was moulding for myself was again being put into the hands of the Master Potter. Eight months of chemotherapy and one month of radiotherapy followed. During this time I was overwhelmed by the displays of God's love through His people, not only to me but also to my family. Prayer support was never-ending, indeed some of which I will never know. As children of God we do not qualify for a life without the physical and emotional pains and stresses of sickness. But we can however be encouraged and comforted in the knowledge that we have a God who loves us immeasurably and is the ultimate and the only source for strength and comfort during such times. Indeed as David writes in Psalm, 18:30, 'He is a shield for all who take refuge in Him'."

David's mother writes, *"David started back to university on 5th February, and has completed his degree with a 2.1 in management and economics. At present he is having a year out but volunteering with Macmillan Cancer Relief and working with children with learning disabilities."*
When the storms of life beat on the frail bark of our lives, it is important to have an anchor.

The Happy Man

Happy is the man whose strength is in God;
For he has resources unseen
To call on when sorrow has swept his frail barque
On the shores of life's turbulent sea:
As the waves of adversity beat on his craft;
High billows their anger release:
His soul is secure in the strength of his God -
He fears not the wrath of the sea!

Happy is the man whose strength is in God;
For he has a fountain within
To spring up when hatred has dried love's clear stream
'Till fear reigns where trust had once been:
As the frost of the wind eats into his soul
Devouring the fruits of God's Grace:
Happy the man whose strength is in God -
This joy springs up fresh from within!

Strength to Cope in Every Situation

READING   2 Corinthians 12: 7-10 and Hebrews 4: 14-16

'My grace is sufficient for you,
for My strength is made perfect in weakness'.   *2 Corinthians 12: 9*

You may have lifted 'Daily Nuggets of Truth' with a sense of weakness. It could be weakness because you are recuperating from an illness or recent surgery, weakness because you face a difficult situation; it could be weakness because you fear the future - or just a feeling that you can't cope. Whatever your situation, God comes to you with His words of assurance - 'My Grace is sufficient for you'.

Raymond had major surgery for cancer at the age of forty-three. When I went to see him hoping I would be able to give him words of comfort and strength to encourage him, I was blessed by his attitude to the future. He reminded me of God's sovereign purpose for our lives. He knew the seriousness of his operation, yet his faith in God was strong in the providential purposes of God. Raymond had an inner strength that could only be described as supernatural. My dear friend, God is your helper and will give you His amazing grace for the difficult journey ahead.

All things through Christ who strengthens me

"All things through Christ
Who strengthens me";
Promise of God
I clearly see,
When everything
Around me tries
To crush my spirit,
Until it cries
For help from all
The devil's blows;
Deliverance from
My raging foes.

"I can" - two words
That reaffirm
My trust in Christ
From Whom I learn -
My weakness gives
A chance to move
With God in faith -
His promise prove!
He cannot fail,
So why should I?
There's work to do
Which I must try.

"All things", must mean
My daily chores;
Cooking the food
When I am bored;
The jobs that need
The extra grace;

The child who comes
With dirty face,
And greasy hands
That leave dark marks:
The neighbour's dog,
Who always barks!

"Through Christ," who died
To make me free,
And rose o'er death
Triumphantly!
The One who sits
At God's right Hand
Who has for me
A pattern planned:
Praise God that in
Temptation's hour,
He victory has
O'er satan's power!

"Who strengthens me" -
Oh blessed thought!
He understands
When I'm distraught!
He knows my cares
And worries too,
And says, 'Fear not,
I'll see you through':
Promise of God -
I'll to you cling -
Through Christ, I'm able
For everything!

The Cruelty of Man to Man

READING   Exodus 1

'Then the king of Egypt spoke to the Hebrew midwives, of whom the name of one was Shiphrah, and the name of the other Puah: and he said 'When you do the duties of a midwife for the Hebrew women and see them on the birthstools, if it is a son, then you shall kill him, but if it is a daughter, then she shall live'   Exodus 1: 15:16

Why are men so cruel?

Why are men so cruel
when superior they are
to animals that roam the fields
and fish that swim the sea?
Men plot and plan such deeds of crime,
treat human life so cheap,
while animals protect their kind -
oft' fight to save and keep!

Why are men so cruel
when God places such a price
upon his soul and values him -
much more than all the world?
He sent His son to Calvary
to suffer awful pain
that man should live in dignity
and one day with Him reign!

We have only to look into the story of human history to see the awful depths to which man can go in cruelty towards his fellow man. War crimes are horrendous! The fact that there is war at all shows us the depravity of our human nature. But the reality is that sin has brought about all the wars of both Biblical times and the wars of succeeding generations. What is so cruel about war is the fact that individuals who go out with a sense of dignity and knowledge of skilled warfare, take crime into their own hands and brutally treat a fellow human. What depth of depravity and cruelty! What horribly twisted mentality! Humanly speaking, there are no answers.

But when we turn to the pages of scripture, we discover the remedy.

As Charles Wesley wrote - 'There is a way for man to rise to that sublime abode, an offering and a sacrifice, a Holy Spirit's energies, an Advocate with God'. Jesus Christ died to redeem man from the fall and there is an advocacy in the atonement for the individual to rise from the depths of his fallen nature to fellowship with God. Yes, we will still face the ravages of war, but hopefully, with individuals changed it will be lawful and not carnal and savage. There is no excuse for man's savage nature to be released on that of another fellow individual. God will hold each accountable!

In 1 Corinthians 13 we discover a better way. Paul writes, 'desire a more excellent way - the way of love! We may have all the achievements that education can produce. We may be orators with tremendous powers of persuasive speech. We may soar in the fields of politics, science and art; we may have an abundance of natural gifts, but if we do not have love, we are 'sounding brass and a tinkling cymbal'. If we do not have love, the Bible says, we have nothing! Jealousy and hatred must be acknowledged and repented of, otherwise they will fester and could lead to murder - could even mean a time behind bars for crimes not intended, but which are sadly the outcome of an evil heart.

Promise of a brighter future
'... the word of the Lord...' 'He shall judge between many peoples. And rebuke strong nations afar off; They shall beat their swords into plowshares, And their spears into pruning hooks; Nation shall not lift up sword against nation, neither shall they learn war any more.' Micah 4:2b:3

95

God Can Become Real to Children

READING   1 Samuel 3: 1-21

Speak Lord for your servant hears.   *1 Samuel 3: 9*

*M*any children, even those as young as four or five years of age, have testified to a knowledge of God and an understanding of His dealing with them. It is important to teach a child to pray and to instruct him from an early age.

A good friend of mine asked me to write a poem for her to teach her Sunday School class for Parents' Night. The result was the following simple poem which you may wish to use as a guideline to teach the children you tuck into bed at night...

Julie-Ann Trounton

Goodnight!

I kneel at my bed at the end of the day
and I know Jesus listens when I start to pray:
I tell Him I'm sorry for things I do wrong,
then ask Him to give me a faith that is strong!
I pray for my Mummy and my Daddy too
- O God I am happy that they both know You:
Bless them and help them to look after me,
make beds and wash dishes, cook dinner and tea:
When Daddy is driving on those busy roads,
keep him safe from all danger - from trucks with big loads!

Bless Grannie and Grandpa, who are both very old
and my little brother who has just caught a cold:
I can't think of anything else I can say...
But really I did have a very good day
- You helped me at school and there wasn't a fight
between those two big bullies
who both think they're right!
Forgive them for all the wrong things they do
and show them that Jesus can make them brand new!
Dear God I pray that You'll help me to sleep,
as under my blankets I'll now softly creep:
Put into my mind the thoughts that are right,
- so God, till the morning, I wish You **goodnight!**

In Harmony With God and Man

READING   Genesis 1

'The flowers appear on the earth; the time of singing has come,
and the voice of the turtledove is heard in our land.'   Song of Solomon: 2: 12

*H*ave you ever wakened to the dawn chorus? To hear the 'chitter - chatter' of a myriad of birds as they both entertain each other and harmoniously communicate by note and sound, is music to the human ear. No composition of music can compare with the diversity in pitch, tone and sound produced by birds as the first tinges of daylight adorn the morning sky. Those who have studied the music of birds stagger us with their information as to the scale of their repertoire of notes recognisable in the best of the world's music. How clever! How perfect is God's creation!

What can we learn from the sweet music of bird song? First and most important, we learn that 'man's chief end is to glorify God and enjoy Him'. Every morning the birds set us an example in praise and worship to the Creator. They never begin a day without songs of praise - and neither should we! If we don't praise Him, the Psalmist David says, 'the very stones cry out'.

The other important lesson we can learn from the dawn chorus is that of fellowship with the people of God. Birds start each day as a community - a 'bird family time of togetherness'! Thus they are in harmony with both God and each other. Surely this was in the original plan and purpose of God for mankind!

But sadly, it all went wrong when Adam and Eve sinned in the Garden of Eden. Thank God that provision has been made through the atoning sacrifice of the Lord Jesus Christ He has opened up a new and living way - 'atonement' simply means 'at one with God'. We can rise to new life in Christ and start each new day in fellowship with God and man. Make a new start today. Determine to rise with praise to God, not just on a Sunday in the place of worship, but daily as you go out to face a cold and hostile world that has no time for the God we love and serve. You will find a whole new dimension to your Christian life!

Dawn

As God rolls back the mantle of night,
Bringing the first rays of sun into sight:
As from its slumber all nature awakes,
So the first note of the dawn chorus breaks;
Each bird chirps its own melodious song,
Then drifts into harmony; before very long
The air is filled with a volume of praise,
While to the Creator, their anthem they raise.

When God rolls back sin's mantle of night,
And to my conscience the Spirit brings light;
As from its slumber my dead soul awakes,
Through all my nature a melody breaks
To Jesus my Saviour, to whom I belong,
My voice joins all nature in jubilant song
You came from the Glory, sinners to save
And triumphed victorious over the grave!

When God rolls back earth's mantle of night
And Christ descends in great splendour and light;
Then from its slumber the world He awakes,
As from the four corners, the redeemed ones He takes;
Oh, what a moment, by the Church waited long,
When we shall be raptured - the resurrection morn!
Loved ones united, together to gaze -
On the face of the Saviour - forever to praise!

Hurt

READING   Matthew 5: 1-12

*'Blessed are you when they revile and persecute you, and say
all kinds of evil against you falsely for My sake. Rejoice
and be exceedingly glad, for great is your reward in heaven...'*   Matthew 5: 11,12

*H*as someone tried to ruin your reputation because of your stand
for truth? Has someone hurt you deeply?

When we read the first twelve verses of Matthew chapter five, we can picture
the Saviour seated on the hillside overlooking Galilee and teaching His disciples.
The beautiful poetry, we know as 'The Beatitudes', climaxes in two amazing
truths - firstly, we are blessed (happy) when people say all kinds of evil against
us falsely when we stand for truth. Secondly, we are to rejoice and be exceeding
glad for we shall have a great reward in heaven. What an amazing revelation!

If you have been treated wrongly for the sake of truth, this is good news for you.
Take your hurt to the Lord and ask Him to heal the wound, take away the
bitterness, help you to forgive those who treated you wrongly and leave the
consequences to Him.

HURT

*When people hurt you, the best thing to do
is go to the Saviour
and battle it through.
He knows the wound and the hurt that you feel,
therefore, be open
and nothing conceal.
Often His purpose is just that we make
a bridge out of trouble
- for there's no mistake
in what God is planning to work for our good
- so just claim His promise
for 'spiritual food'.*

Very often we can see a greater plan for our lives through the difficult experience
of having been treated wrongly. It is never easy to 'turn the other cheek', but if
we do God brings us into a deeper relationship with Him.

Let go of your resentment and allow God to heal it. Next time you meet the person who has wronged you, greet him with a genuine warmth - it will bring you tremendous blessing and release the hurt!

Tears and Joy

Grief pierces the heart
like an arrow on target to kill:
It brings in its wake
pain and sorrow-
An emptiness nothing can fill!
But tears are the language of sorrow,
expressing the heart's inner grief,
then cleansing and healing emotions-
restoring and bringing relief.
Joy gladdens the heart
like a bird released from its cage:
It breaks into song, sometimes laughter-
dispels gloominess, sorrow or rage:
Tears can be the language of gladness,
expressing a freedom from care-
or sharing life's blessings with others
tears help us our hearts to make bare.

When a Nation Becomes Great

READING   2 Chronicles 7

'Righteousness exalts a nation,
but sin is a reproach to any people.'   *Proverbs 14: 34*

*G*reen, in his "History of the English People', said, 'No greater moral change ever passed over a nation than passed over England during the years which parted the middle of the reign of Elizabeth, from the meeting of the Long Parliament. England became the people of a book, and that book was the Bible'. After speaking of the 'loftiness and ardour of expression' which the Scriptures gave to the literature of that time, Green continues, "'But far greater than its effect on literature or social phrase was the effect of the Bible on the character of the people at large... One dominant influence told on human action. The whole temper of the nation felt the change. A new conception of life and of man superseded the old. A new moral and religious impulse spread through every class...'

Today we have a sad situation in Britain. With the increase in knowledge, which Jesus said would happen before His return to earth, has come a relaxation in our laws - in fact, we have gone back to the sins that caused God's wrath to be poured out on Sodom and Gomorrah, the same sins the Apostle Paul denounced in the first chapter of Romans. As our nation sinks lower and lower morally, one wonders what God will have to do to bring us to our knees.

At the dedication of the temple, when Solomon finished praying, 'fire came down from heaven and consumed the burnt offering and the sacrifices, and the glory of the Lord filled the temple.' When the Israelites saw the fire coming down from heaven and the glory of the Lord above the temple, they knelt on the pavement with their faces to the ground and worshipped and gave thanks to the Lord. When Solomon had finished the temple and the royal palace, the Lord appeared to him and said, 'I have heard your prayer and have chosen this place for Myself as a temple for sacrifice.' But God's people were not ready for what He was going to do. They had to repent, before He could pour out His blessing and lead them forward to new avenues of victory.

God said, 'When I shut up heaven and there is no rain, or command the locusts to devour the land or send pestilence among My people, if My people, who are called by My name, will humble themselves and pray and seek my face and turn from their wicked ways, then will I hear from heaven, and will forgive their sin and heal their land.'   2 Chronicles 7: 13,14

God's pattern does not change. He still requires repentance of sin and humility of attitude, whether it is an individual or a nation. Has our nation taken note of the tragedy of the Foot and Mouth plague?   Bishop Ryle wrote, during a previous outbreak of the disease, warning our nation. From scripture he pointed out that this was indeed the judgement of God. Have we put the experience of Britain's most serious outbreak of Foot and Mouth disease 'under the carpet' and gone further down the 'slippery slope' of moral decline? The history of the nation of Israel is a tragic one. They were a very special people whom God raised up for His purpose and glory. But their rejection of the Messiah has had its effect on their whole history. In His divine purpose, God brought the Jews back to become a nation again in 1948. Since that, their turbulent history has continued until this present day. Is God shaping up things for the return of His Son and the fulfilment of scripture for the end of time?

God's Call to Israel

Wayward nation, I will heal you
if you will repent of sin;
Come with heart and deep contrition -
favoured race,
My smile you'll win:
I will graciously receive you -
have compassion on your race,
though you turned from Me to idols
I extend to you MY GRACE!

Wayward nation I will love you
if you will acknowledge Me!
With a heart that's true and contrite -
I will set your people free!
I will be like dew to Israel
ransom and redeem from death,
you will grow up like the lily
I'll give life to barren earth!

continued over

Wayward nation, I will bless you -
you will flourish like the grain,
blossom like the vine or lily
when I give the latter rain:
I will water barren Israel -
men will dwell again in shade,
from the cedar trees in Lebanon
fragrance once again I'll shed.

Wayward nation, turn to Jesus -
your Messiah - KING OF KINGS!
He was God, the Son incarnate -
let us all our homage bring!
then with 'saints' from all the ages
who have found in Christ the Way,
we shall reign with Him in glory -
in the realms of endless day!

(Based on the book of Hosea).

The same call is applicable to God's spiritual Israel - the Church. As a church, we have grown cold in our love and dedication to Him. We have sinned and need to repent and seek the Lord's forgiveness: as a church we have made idols - perhaps not of wood and stone, but idols of self-indulgence, of materialism, of our own ego. Personally and collectively, we need to come back to God and allow Him to cleanse and forgive our sin and turn our hearts to righteousness. He is calling us to humility, prayer and repentance. Then He will be faithful to His promise and will heal our land and forgive our personal sin and our national sin. Let us heed God through the prophet Hosea and know His healing!

Majesty in Prayer

READING   2 Chronicles 20: 1-30

'Jehoshaphat feared, and set himself to seek the Lord...'
'Jehoshaphat stood in the congregation of Judah and Jerusalem,
in the house of the Lord, before the new court...'   *2 Chronicles 20: 3,5*

*O*ld Testament prayers are powerful because they don't start with the problem or need. It is interesting to note that they begin by focusing on the character and attributes of God. Our praying is usually very different in that we normally begin by telling God about our problem. A great prayer is that of David at the dedication of the temple, when practically the whole prayer is one of acknowledging the attributes and character of God. It reminds us of His greatness, His power, His glory! There are only two requests in the whole prayer - one for the people that they will never forget the experience and the other for Solomon, his son, that he would have a perfect heart and keep the commandments and obey the Lord.

Jehoshaphat's prayer sets guidelines for all our prayers, including intercessory prayer. The king begins by recognising God, as the God of truth. He makes a statement and asks a question. He declares that 'God is the God of our fathers' and reminds God and those who listen to his prayer, of past deliverance. This approach does two things - it inspires the people and it encourages personal faith. Jehoshaphat is basically saying, God can do it! He is taking his hands off the situation and recognising the power of the God of Israel who has performerd miracles for His people in the past and will do it again. History can inspire us for the future - try this and you will discover that such an approach will bring a change of attitude to your prayer. Pause and thank God for how He answered prayer in the past. This will take you to a new level of faith - for the God who heard you in the past, is the same yesterday, today and forever. Will He fail you in this situation?

If the request isn't right, His answer is '**no**'!
If the timing isn't right, His answer is '**slow**'!
If you aren't ready yet, His answer is '**grow**'!
When everything's ready and right, His answer is '**go**'!

Growing Through Struggle

READING   1 Samuel 20

'They wept together, but David more so...'   *1 Samuel 20: 41*

*T*he story of the friendship between Jonathan and David is one of the most remarkable stories of loyalty and growth of friendship through struggles imaginable. When one realises that it was Jonathan's father, Saul, who wanted to kill David, and 'blood is thicker than water' says the proverb, it was a courageous step taken by Jonathan to protect David.

Saul was jealous of David because he was chosen by God to be king. Saul, no doubt, wanted his son to rule after him, which was his motive for seeking to kill David. It would have been understandable if Jonathan had taken sides with his father, but the young man feared God, and, knowing that 'an evil spirit' had entered into Saul, he did what was right in the circumstances - his fear of God was more important than his own life. What a struggle he must have had! That struggle is not recorded, but we know that both Jonathan and David battled with inner conflicts and conquered their fear in order to obey God.

Their struggle deepened their friendship and young Jonathan risked his life for his friend. We may not be called on to risk our lives but in the race towards the 'prize for the high calling of God in Christ Jesus', we daily face battles and struggles. All the satanic forces of hell are arrayed against the Christian in our hostile world. We do, and should 'stick out like a sore thumb'! It costs! But the reward is eternal and the prize is big - much bigger than anything the world can offer. It is 'a crown of righteousness'. Let us then face the struggles and fight the Lord's battles! We are victors before we start because the victory over Satan was won at Calvary.

Dr J. R. Millar wrote: 'The nominal Christian life that costs nothing is not worthy of the name! There must be self-restraint, discipline, severe schooling. There must be struggle, the agonising effort. If you are to reach the goal and win the prize, you must put the energy of your life into the race. There must be sacrifice of indolence and self-will and personal ease. Too much pampering spoils many an earnest Christian. Every noble life is a struggle from beginning to end; only those who resist and fight and overcome are successful in life. This is true in every sphere - in business, in study, in professional life, and in spiritual life. Are we resisting sin, overcoming temptation, living victoriously in trial? If not, we are not living worthily'.

Refreshment for the Soldier

Weary traveller in the desert
thirsting for a water spring
lift your eyes to yon oasis -
it will health and healing bring:
All the depth of secret longing,
it will quickly satisfy:
Haste, Oh haste, dear weary traveller -
Quench your thirst and drink with joy!

Drowning sailor in the ocean
clutching to a sinking bark,
lift your eyes to yonder lifeboat-
it is just within your grasp.
All the frantic sights of terror
they will be forever past!
Haste, Oh haste, dear drowning sailor
If you linger, you'll be lost!

The Hand of God

READING   Psalm 145

'You open your hand and satisfy the desire of every living thing'.   *Psalm 145: 16*

*T*here are various references in scripture to 'the Hand of God'. One of the most beautiful is our text for today. God's open Hand! God's generosity is characterised by His open hand. Think of it... the God who holds the nation in His hand, the God who created the universe, the God who sent His Son to be the Saviour of the world, opens His hand to us! We just have to look at the birds. Nature provides for them in winter as well as in summer. I often look at the cotoneaster, covered with bright red berries. How pleasant on a cold winter day to watch the birds peck at these. Sometimes a berry will fall to the ground and the little bird sees it and sweeps down to continue feeding. Birds enjoy God's bountiful provision as He opens His hand to feed them.

Hard times may come, but God will provide for His children. Those unexpected gifts, the ability to think of better ways to earn money or the wisdom to be more economical - all this is God's generosity and the opening of His hand to provide for us. God's provision is satisfactory. It may not be luxurious but He satisfies every living creature. In the poverty of communist Russia, peasants had to search through the dumps with birds of prey for food. One Christian man found a crust of bread   He cut off the mildew and put it into his bag to bring home. But what satisfaction there was on his face because of his find. He gave thanks to God for opening His hand and providing for him. (Perhaps we should be thinking more about those who are in need and opening our hands to our brother!)

Besides the provision for our needs, God has shown us kindness in the changing seasons, in giving us the gift of life, in giving us comfort in sorrow, and above all, in giving us the gift of salvation. John tells us that Jesus came to His own people, the Jews, and they did not receive Him, but he goes on to explain that to as many as receive Him, He gives the right to become children of God. John 1: 12. This is the greatest gift anyone could ever receive! It is free and can be obtained when one repents of sin and by faith accepts the atoning death of the Lord Jesus Christ as God's substitute for sin. God has His hand open and offers the sinner His gift of eternal life.

Another aspect of God in respect to His Hands, is the fact that He has made us and fashioned us - Psalm 119:73. What a reassuring thought when one's health is failing; when major surgery looms ahead; when the specialist diagnoses a terminal illness, or when facing the 'valley of the shadow of death'. If you do not understand what is happening in your body, be encouraged that God, who made you and fashioned you, knows your present situation. It has not taken Him by surprise. You are a child of His care and He will not fail you in your hour of need!

You are special to God

You are special to God,
You're a child of His care,
Part of His family,
A son and an heir!
All that the Father
Has given to Christ
Is offered to those
Who have made Him their choice!

You are special to God,
By new-birth you are part
Of His chosen family,
You're dear to His heart!
A member of Christ,
Joint heir to the throne,
One day you will enter
His heavenly home.

You are special to God,
For He bought you with blood,
You are of more value
Than silver or gold!
His Son paid the price
That you might go free
When he suffered and died
On Calvary's tree!

You are special to God,
He has called you by name;
He formed you; Redeemed you;
There's no greater fame
Than to be friend to
Christ Jesus the King,
To be a partaker
Of the blessings that brings!

The Song of Obedience

READING   2 Chronicles 20: 18-29 & Psalm 121

'...when he (Jehosaphat), had consulted with the people, he appointed those who should sing to the Lord, and who should praise the beauty of holiness, as they went out before the army and were saying,
"Praise the Lord, for His mercy endures forever'.   2 Chronicles 20: 21

As the army of the Lord drew nearer to the Ascent of Ziz, it must have been disconcerting for the enemy. A choir marching in front of the army! The sounds would have been indistinguishable in the distance - perhaps they thought it was a strong wind, a storm, or thunder, but as it came near they would have heard the words, *'Praise the Lord for His mercy endures forever.'* How did they react? Wonder! Dread! Fear! Weakness! No doubt there was total disarray! Then the unbelievable sight - the army of Judah was not attacking! They just stood there singing! How could such a thing happen? Nobody could have imagined anything more ludicrous - an army with a choir in front singing and not attacking! The secret was that Judah was obeying the God who controls His world, and even the armies of the world can only go so far - God has the final word. Had He not said... "You will not need to fight in this battle, stand still and see the salvation of the Lord". The result was victory because the armies of Moab were so confounded that they fought among themselves. Judah just watched as they killed each other and when they went over, found the dead bodies of their enemies.

As we look back in history, we have examples of this. What was it that turned the fortune of the British at the Spanish Armada? It was not the inefficiency of the Spanish fleet, nor the superiority of the British, that won the Spanish Armada, because both armies had competent and able naval fleets and commanders. The God who controls the elements of His world was in control. Winds and tides were the key to Britain's success in the English Channel. Unprecedented gales swept across the English Channel making the west coast perilous for the ships that survived. T. P. Kilfeather, an experienced journalist from Sligo, in his book "Ireland Graveyard of the Spanish Armada", writes of an evening in September 1588, off the coast of Ireland, when the Atlantic heaved and surged with pitiless restlessness. Kilfeather describes the scene - 'death was in the screaming of the wind'. Twenty-four, maybe twenty-six ships of the Spanish Armada were wrecked and more than 5,000 men died in what must be one of the greatest sea disasters of history. There are some things beyond the control of even the most experienced seamen and war strategists. Prayer changes things!

Dear Reader, whatever your battle - whether with people, a nation or in your own personal life, reckon on God's intervention. If you have committed your cause to Him, then do not be surprised if He 'works in mysterious ways, His wonders to perform'. Perhaps you have already won the battle! Now it is a case of ... "stand still and see the salvation of the Lord".

Trust

To turn away from earthly things
  And taste the comfort that it brings
    To rest beneath almighty wings -
      This is trust.

To walk so closely at His side
  That I can lean upon my Guide
    In safety, whatsoe'r betide -
      This is trust.

To roll on Him the load of care
  That grows too wearisome to bear
    And gladly learn to leave it there -
      This is trust.

To stay the heart and soul and mind
  Upon my Lord and thus to find
    The perfect peace He has designed -
      This is trust.

Jean Corbett

The Blessing of Friendship

READING   1 Samuel 20

'Then Jonathan said to David, "Go in peace,
since we have both sworn in the name of the Lord, saying,
'May the Lord be between you and me, and between
your descendants and my descendants, forever'."   *1 Samuel 20: 42*

The gift of friendship is a very special blessing. In chapters nineteen and twenty of the first book of Samuel, we have an account of one of the most amazing friendships between two people. It is particularly significant when we realise that Jonathan was Saul's son and David was the enemy of Saul. We can picture the scene when Abner and David return from the battle - David carrying the head of the giant. Instead of gratitude, Saul is jealous of David, but as young Jonathan looks on, he, no doubt is filled with admiration. What the army of Israel could not do, David had achieved. No wonder David was Jonathan's hero! His look of admiration was short-lived for he detected his father's attitude. Was there conflict in the young man's mind? This we do not know, but if there was, the decision was made in favour of the young hero, David. Chapter eighteen opens with Jonathan making a covenant with David. He took off the robe he was wearing and gave it to David along with his tunic, and even his sword, his bow and his belt. Would Jonathan's loyalty remain when the pressure grew and the people danced and sang, 'Saul has slain his thousands, and David his tens of thousands'?

As the story continues we see the bond between Jonathan and David strengthen. Saul's anger became so great that he decided to kill David. Jonathan discovered the plot and told David. A way of escape was devised. The first attempt Saul made on David's life was while he was playing his harp. Saul knew his routine and planned his death with a spear. The attempt failed! The next plot to get the admiration of Israel and Judah away from the young hero was to offer David his daughter Marabou, in marriage with the condition that he would serve him. Saul had plans for David to be killed in battle but again his plot failed. As the story continues the more Saul's hatred for David grew, the stronger the bonds of friendship developed between Jonathan and David. Chapter twenty is an amazing narrative of love, loyalty and genuine friendship.

No doubt as you meditate on this account of a remarkable friendship, you think of the wonderful friends you have - those whose trust you have proved and whose friendship is very special. Pause to thank God for those good friends and, above all, thank Him for 'the friend that sticks closer than a brother' - the Lord Jesus Christ.

Friendship

For friendship that weathers the battles of life
   in a world that is full of hatred and strife -
      this I will treasure, such friends can be found,
         though I know there are many who do let you down.

For friendship that weathers the critics of mine,
   you often have spoken a word that is kind:
      When someone has torn my reputation to shreds -
         you, friend, have been there, together we prayed.

For friendship that weathers my different moods,
   you don't hold resentment, nor let your thoughts brood
      on something that wasn't intended to be
         a wedge in a friendship, that's special to me.

For friendship that weathers the passing of years -
   one that has deepened through joys and through tears:
      Intimate thoughts only shared with a few -
         I often thank God I could share them with you.

The Greatest Event in History

READING   John 1: 1-12

'He came to His own and His own did not
receive Him, but as many as received Him,
to them He gave the right to become children of God...'   *John 1: 11,12*

There is no doubt about the fact that the coming of the Saviour - the Lord Jesus Christ was the greatest event in the history of the world. His appearance on earth is the central event of world history, and His uniqueness is seen in that after the passage of over 2,000 years, His birth, death and resurrection are universally recognised. Such was the impact that it changed the calendar - History before His birth is B.C. and after His birth is A.D. - Anno Domini, the year of **our Lord.** Those who reduce Christ to the level of ordinary humanity find it difficult to explain how He could be important enough to divide world history.

LECKY, in his 'History of European Morals' has this remarkable tribute to Christ's influence upon history - 'It was reserved for Christianity to present to the world an ideal character... and the simple record of three short years of active life has done more to regenerate and soften mankind than all the writings of philosophers and all the exhortations of moralists.' In collating all the WRITTEN WORD unfolds of Him who became the LIVING WORD, it has been set thus: 'More than 2000 years ago there was a Man born contrary to the laws of life. This Man lived in poverty and was reared in obscurity... 'Only once did He cross the boundary of the country in which He lived: that was during His exile in childhood... 'In infancy He startled a king: in childhood He puzzled the doctors: in manhood He ruled the course of nature, walked upon the billows as if on pavement, and hushed the sea to sleep. 'He never wrote a book, and yet all of the libraries of the country could not hold the books that have been written about Him. 'He never wrote a song, and yet He has furnished the theme for more songs than all the song writers combined. 'He never founded a college, but all the schools put together cannot boast of having as many students... 'The names of the past proved statesmen of Greece and Rome have come and gone. The names of the past scientists, philosophers and theologians have come and gone; but the name of this Man abounds more and more. 'Though time has spread over 2000 years between the people of this generation and scene of His crucifixion, yet He still lives. Herod could not destroy Him, and the grave could not hold Him.

'He stands forth upon the highest pinnacle of Heavenly glory, proclaimed of God, acknowledged by angels, adored by saints, and feared by devils, as the living, personal Christ, our Lord and our God.'

FURTHER: In his 'A Portrait of Jesus', Sherwood Eddy pays this beautiful tribute to His remarkable character and influence - 'Jesus left no book, no tract or written page behind Him. He bequeathed no system, no philosophy, no theology, no legislation. He raised no armies, organised no institutions, held no office, sought no influence. He was no scholar, and yet He is more quoted than any writer in all history. His sayings at times are on almost every tongue, and his words have literally gone out into the world. No man ever laid down his life in Asia or in Africa to translate Plato or Aristotle, Kant or Hegel, Shakespeare or Milton, but hundreds have died to carry Jesus' priceless words to the ends of the earth. Several hundred languages have been reduced to writing in order to transmit His life-giving message. Savage tribes have been uplifted, cannibals civilised, head-hunters converted, schools and colleges founded, and the character and culture of individuals and of peoples have been changed as the result of the influence of His words which are creative spirit and life.'

He Came to Earth

Did Jesus have to come to earth,
Be humbled to a lowly birth
In stable bare?
Live here for three and thirty years,
Accept the ridicule and jeers
Of cruel men?
Yes, Jesus had to come to earth,
Even though it meant a cruel death
On Calvary
There was no other way that God
Could justly pardon sinful man,
Cleanse and forgive.
But on the merits of His Son,
The Lamb of God - the Sinless One -
Our Substitute!
He took the place of fallen man,
To make us Kings and Priests to God
And lift the curse!
Thanks be to God
Christ came to earth!

God's Goodness and Man's Wickedness

READING   Psalm 73

'Truly God is good to Israel...'   *Psalm 73: 1*

*T*his was no 'tip of the tongue' utterance, but a conclusion reached after a serious pondering of his own situation and a true assessment of the godless society around him.

Asaph had taken time to weigh up all the facts and laments the seeming success, and the apparent freedom of the godless and the oppression of the people of God. The situation had depressed him. In fact he states - 'my steps had nearly slipped.' He had nearly lost his hold as he questions the prosperity of the wicked, their immunity from struggles and their bodily health. Poetically, he declares - 'Pride serves as their necklace; violence covers them like a garment.' From the outward evidence of freedom, he moves to the inward and secret cause of their godlessness - 'Their eyes bulge with abundance: 'They have more than heart could wish.' Psalm 73: 7. Asaph continues his lament as he describes their speech - 'They scoff and speak wickedly concerning oppression; They speak loftily.' Psalm 73: 8 - He concludes his lengthy declaration by stating, '...these are the ungodly, who are always at ease; 'They increase in riches.' Psalm 73: 12, despite the fact that 'those who are far from God will perish.' Psalm 73: 27. From grovelling in self-pity, fortunately Asaph goes to the house of God and gets things into perspective. He began to understand the ultimate destiny of the wicked. Gradually he emerged from self-pity to pity for the people he had described - their end is destruction, he declares.

Dealing with negative emotions can be a painful experience. Asaph had to deal with the sin of envy and the despair of self-pity. He had lost his grip on God and found himself reasoning without taking the higher and spiritual plan into account. While we remain in a fallen world, this temptation will always be present. Whatever spiritual heights we may aspire to, there will always be conflict. Like Peter, if we take our eyes off the Master of every circumstance, we sink. The only place of safety is to keep following the Lord, keep our priorities right and walk humbly with our God. Ultimately, the wicked will meet their end with remorse and everlasting separation from God but the righteous will inherit eternal life and reward.

God Knows

There is the wicked and there is the scoffer
There is the pauper with nothing to offer:
There are the proud and there goes the boaster:
There is envy - a horrible monster!
Here is the godly and here is the truthful:
Here is the honest and here is the faithful!

Misunderstood

READING   John 19

'But they cried out,
"Away with Him!... we have no king but Caesar!"   John 19: 15

*E*ver felt you were misunderstood? Of course your answer is 'yes'.
Everyone has been hurt by being misinterpreted when a certain twist given either to one's words or actions has conveyed a different meaning. Be encouraged, for the Saviour has experienced it too. When He declared His deity, the crowd became furious - they expected an earthly king who would set up His kingdom and begin His rule on earth. There was no way that Jesus Christ, the humble man from Nazareth, would meet their expectations, so they cried, 'Away with Him, we do not want this man to rule over us - Crucify Him!" Even among His followers, there was a desire for power. They wanted to know how they would fare in His kingdom. Who would be the greatest? The purpose of the Saviour was completely misunderstood for He knew He would not be with them and needed to prepare them for leadership. But the disciples misread his purpose and had position in their thinking.

Such was the submission of the Lord Jesus Christ to the Father's will and acceptance of rejection and misunderstanding, that it is written - 'Who when He was reviled, He reviled not again'.

We feel a sense of protection for those in our society who are vulnerable and often become the victims of gross misunderstanding. Has it not been the case that people have jumped to conclusions rather than arrive at them? When we see an injustice in our judicial system and it is obvious to all that the innocent party has suffered, we want to cry out in protest, but our words are futile. Eventually, we just accept and know that ultimately, God will mete out the justice. You may be reading this today and feel you have been treated unfairly - Take your hurt to the Lord for He understands. He was treated unfairly by His own people. He came to the Jewish nation as their Messiah and they rejected Him. He still comes to Jew and Gentile and the cry goes up - 'We don't want this man to rule over us!'

Throughout my life, I have felt pain when I have watched people cringe in agony because of an injustice or a misunderstanding. They have struggled to keep calm and not retaliate; they have decided to leave it with the Lord and not fight for their rights. How admirable! I salute you!

'Have we no Rights' by Mildred Cable and Francisca French is a book that sadly is out of print. The writer's thorough examination of the subject and logical conclusions greatly influenced my thinking. I do not find it easy, but I have proved that in those times when I have been the innocent party and accepted an injustice, it has enriched my spiritual life and given me an identity with the many who have experienced a similar hurt.

Misunderstood

Misunderstood by friends you thought dear;
misunderstood just because it's not clear
what you're trying to do for the Saviour you love
and who reveals secrets from heaven above.

Misunderstood it's the way of the Cross;
misunderstood, counting all things but dross;
save the assurance, God's purpose is clear
and His presence is with you to cast out all fear!

No Basis For a Charge

READING   John 19

*'Pilate said to them, "You take Him
and crucify Him, for I find no fault in Him."*   *John 19: 6b*

*P*ilate wriggled to free himself from a difficult situation! But, despite the fact that he tried to wash his hands of Jesus, he was guilty. Like a spineless jelly fish, he tried to bury his guilt by placing the responsibility on the crowd.

But as you study John's account of the story, you discover Pilate was placed in a very awkward situation. As far as he was concerned, accusations had been made that he had to deal with and be seen to do justice. Although Jesus said, '...the one who handed Me over to you is guilty of a greater sin', Pilate was not innocent of the dreadful punishment and death of the Saviour. In verse one of John nineteen, we read - 'Then Pilate took Jesus and had him flogged'. What dreadful punishment on the innocent Son of God! Those who have visited that dungeon and had the 'flogging procedure' explained in detail, know the awful suffering inflicted on the Saviour of the world. He was flogged with a leather thong that tore his flesh until it 'was like a ploughed field'; then left until he survived a beating and was able to feel the next one - this procedure was repeated until the victim could take no more. Oh the cruelty of man to man! Where Jesus was concerned, prophecy was fulfilled, as predicted by Isaiah, 'I gave my back to those who beat Me...' *Isaiah, 50:6.* To the man whom Pilate could find no charge against, the punishment of Jesus was unbelievable. After the flogging, the soldiers twisted together a crown of thorns and put it on His head. Those thorns were not like our small thorns in the hedgerows, but large thorns some several inches long with sharp piercing points - these were plaited and probably pressed into the Saviour's head to cause severe pain and bleeding. I wonder which of those soldiers actually twisted and formed the crown?

Pardoned

The Crown of Thorns

I wonder who plaited the crown of thorns
that pierced the Saviour's head,
was he there to see the blood flow down,
as Christ to the cross was led?
Did he see Him bend 'neath His heavy load?
Did he watch them drive in the nails?
Was he proud to have made the crown of thorns
that pierced the Saviour's head?

I wonder if he who made the crown
that pierced the Saviour's head,
was there to see His awful death
and hear the words He prayed'?
'Father, forgive them,' He breathed through His pain,
as the crowd mocked the Son of God:
Did he wish he had never made the crown
that pierced the Saviour's head?

I wonder if he who made the crown
that pierced the Saviour's brow,
could speak to us now of the crown he made,
- would have regrets and say
'I went with the throng, not knowing the wrong,
my conscience is plagued with guilt:
If only I had never made the crown
that pierced the Saviour's head?

If this account of the torture inflicted on one human being by another was just a historic event that we commemorated at Easter, we would find it moving and add it to the barbarous beatings and killings of others throughout history. But this was the greatest event in history for God was fulfilling His plan for a lost world. Jesus Christ was the sinless Son of God, was with God before the world began and 'God so loved the world that He gave His only begotten Son that whoever believes on Him should not perish but have everlasting life'. Jesus was the Messiah and the Saviour of the world and all the prophecies of the Old Testament were fulfilled in His suffering and death at Calvary. He died an atoning death for me!

Just one vital question for you today - Have you appropriated that atoning death? Have you received Christ as your personal Saviour and Lord? If you have, then give Him thanks again for such a supreme sacrifice on your behalf and go out to share the Good News with others.

Gone But Not Forgotten

READING   Psalm 15

*'Lord, who may abide in Your tabernacle...?' He who walks uprightly,
and works righteousness, and speaks the truth in his heart:'*   Psalm 15: 1a & 2

*M*any of the world's heroes have never been recognised by their country's leaders or recorded in history for their significant contribution to society. In fact many have been forgotten by all but their immediate family. The character of the Bible's greatest hero is described in our Psalm for today. It is challenging to read it and apply it to our living. It deals with our walk in righteousness and truth and with our speech and behaviour, it deals with our attitude to others and it covers our use of money. Such heroes must never be forgotten!

I talked recently to a widow who told me that this was her late husband's favourite Psalm. Carroll Bell was an architect with the Education Authorities. Among the many buildings he designed for the Education Board was Killicomaine Junior High School in Portadown, Co Armagh, N. Ireland. Carroll was a talented man not only in architecture, but also in music and in his work with the Heart and Chest Foundation - in these fields he made a valuable contribution as a church organist and a tireless worker with the local branch of the Chest and Heart Foundation. He frequently read Psalm fifteen, and no doubt, sought to apply it to his daily living. But when Carroll was diagnosed with a terminal illness, he made this lovely little Psalm, his 'Daily Bread'. His wife's lasting memory of him is of a devoted husband and father sitting up in bed reading his favourite Psalm.

What is so special about the Psalm? Surely it must be the heart-searching challenge! It cuts right across our twenty-first century's behaviour and thinking. Walking uprightly, speaking the truth, honouring those who fear the Lord, and not using money for bribery and corruption, are not the hallmarks of our living today.

Those who seek to live to the standards of God's Word will never be forgotten!

Memories

Wave upon wave, relentless and unceasing
Memories break on thought's defenceless shore,
Each bearing tribute from time's varied storehouse
Hidden in ocean depths long years before.

Gay little wavelets sparkling in sunshine
Dancing because of happiness they bring
From countless blessings sent, though all unworthy
- By the great Giver of each joyous thing.

Great crashing breakers lashed to wildest fury
By memories of storms long since endured,
Leaving, even now, an ache of desolation
Within the wounds that only God has cured.

Lord of the waves who walks on the water,
Grant that when memories break on this thronged shore,
Whatever they may bring, may they returning,
Bear precious treasure for tomorrow's store.

Jean Corbett

The Power of the Holy Spirit

READING   Acts 1: 1-9

'You shall receive power when the Holy Spirit has come upon you...'   *Acts 1: 8*

After the crucifixion of the Lord Jesus Christ, the disciples were not only fearful of the Jews but they were powerless. Someone has described them as a modern motor car without petrol. Where would they go from here? The Saviour had gone from view and they had no idea of what the future held. Had they not left their trade or profession to follow 'the lone Nazarene? Was their sacrifice in vain? Should the fishermen just go back to their fishing nets, Luke to his medical profession, Matthew to his tax collecting etc? Had they all become redundant? No doubt, they remembered the words of Jesus in Luke 24:49 - 'Stay in the city until you receive power from on high'. Did they doubt His promise'? Had they lost faith? We do not know the thoughts and questions that went through their minds, but they must have wondered how such a thing could happen. In obedience they waited. In the opening chapters of Acts, we are introduced to the most significant and dramatic event since the death, resurrection and ascension of the Saviour. They were all gathered, as the Lord had commanded, waiting for something to happen - and happen it did! Just as Jesus had promised the Holy Spirit came and the disciples were transformed from timid individuals to powerful men of God who changed the face of history. Pentecost had far reaching effects. The New Testament Church was born and has grown for more than two thousand years. Some commentators suggest that Pentecost was the fulfilment of the prophecy of the Lord Jesus Christ in Mark's gospel... 'for some standing here will not taste death before they see the kingdom of God come with power.' **Mark 9: 1.**   We do know that as a result of Pentecost, Christianity spread throughout the entire Roman Empire.

That Kingdom is still growing. The fact that it is not growing in the west, does not mean it is not growing elsewhere. In fact, it is growing at a phenomenal rate in what has been called 'the third world'. Sadly, our materialism, apathy and secularism have curtailed the spread of the Gospel in Britain - now we have a godless society. One fears that God's judgement and wrath will be poured out on our nation if we do not repent. If we go deeper into the sins that brought judgement on Sodom and Gomorrah, God may have to allow something drastic to happen. Our nation needs to get back to the Bible that was the secret of England's greatness during the reign of Queen Victoria.

Those who object, criticise the 'dos' and 'don'ts' of the Victorian era, but God only puts prohibitions on us for our own good and the future of our race. We do not go back to the culture of the Victorian era, which some of us would find objectionable, but we do have to go back to the morality of the Victorian era. That is totally acceptable to me and I personally would welcome it! In fact God demands it from His Word and therefore - WE MUST PREACH IT? What about the spiritual needs in the Republic of Ireland? Unfortunately, the vacuum left from the failure of Roman Catholicism is being filled with materialism and this beautiful island too faces God's judgement and wrath. But there is hope for our fellow-countrymen because, sadly, they did not have the Word of God until the past two or three decades. We know there are many who are seeking the truth of God's Word and our prayer is that we, in the Church of Jesus Christ, will be so filled with the Holy Ghost that God can use us to bring truth, light and love to those who are in darkness. God is just and therefore cannot judge a people kept in darkness, with the same judgement as those who have once had the light and wilfully rejected it.

The Call of Ireland

Over the hills and the valleys
of this our Island so fair:
Out in the highways and byways -
men live and die in despair:
Groping for light in their darkness,
seeking release from their fear
wandering alone on the mountains -
their burdens too heavy to bear!

Who'll tell these lost ones of Jesus?
Who'll go today at His call?
Leaving their ease and their comfort
yielding to Jesus their all.

Shadows are gathering o'er Erin -
night closes in all around:
Who then will carry the message
to those who in darkness are bound?
Soon 'open doors' will be closing!
Soon will the Master appear!
Haste then to carry the Gospel -
to those who are groping in fear.

'Also I heard the voice
of the Lord saying:
"Whom shall I send,
and who will go for us?"
Then I said
"Here am I, send me".
Isaiah 6 v 8

A Change of Mind

READING   Acts 27: 6 - 28: 10

'...they changed their minds and said that he was a god'.   *Acts 28: 6b*

Today we turn our thoughts to a shipwreck on the Adriatic Sea. Although Paul had warned of an impending storm and advised the crew not to venture out on the high seas, they decided to go ahead. Imagine the scene - two hundred and seventy six people caught in a horrific storm. After fourteen days, the ferocious gales had driven them totally off course: there was panic when the sailors took soundings and they realised they were in danger of being dashed on the rocks. They reacted by dropping four anchors and praying for daylight. Then they made an attempt to escape by letting down the lifeboat into the sea. Paul advised the centurion and the soldiers to keep everyone on board and to cut the ropes that held the lifeboat and let it fall away. It must have seemed ridiculous to give such advice, but they obeyed. He assured them that not one of them would be lost. Then the inevitable happened - the boat struck a sand bar and ran aground. The bow stuck and would not move, and the stern was broken to pieces by the pounding surf. Paul ordered those who could swim to jump overboard first and get to land. The rest were to get there on planks or pieces of the ship. They all reached the land safely! When Paul and those on board with him were ship wrecked on the island of Malta, the islanders gave them a warm welcome - because it was wet and cold, they lit a fire and showed unusual kindness. But that was short lived! When Paul gathered a bundle of sticks for the fire and a snake emerged from them and bit him, they accused him of being a murderer. Because the snake bit him, they decided that it was 'justice' for a prisoner. But when Paul shook the snake off into the fire and was not harmed, they changed their minds and said he was a god. How quick they were to judge! How easily they changed their minds!

Man has not changed today - the crowd still changes sides so quickly! The Saviour of the world suffered the same ignominy. As He entered Jerusalem, they were waving palm branches and hailing Him as their king, but they were still crying 'away with Him, crucify Him - we will not have this man to rule over us'! Do not be alarmed if you suffer as a Christian. In fact, Jesus said, 'to count it joy if you suffer for His sake'.

He Pressed On

From Bethlehem's manger to Calvary He went;
The Saviour pressed on!
Exchanging the straw of a stable for wood-
He carried a Cross:
The angels who brought to the shepherds the message,
That Christ the Redeemer was there to behold;
No longer rejoiced as the great King of ages,
Was led to the Cross, as a lamb to the fold:
But Jesus remembered the will of His Father,
And gladly pressed on.

From listening to doctors to judgement He went;
Our Saviour pressed on!
Exchanging the freedom of childhood for death;
He carried our load!
The disciples whose love and friendship had helped Him,
No longer rejoiced, or remembered His call;
Despised and forsaken, the King of all ages;
to His last hour of anguish drank vinegar and gall;
Yes, Jesus remembered the will of His Father:
And gladly pressed on.

From Calvary's shadow to Heaven He went,
My Saviour pressed on!
Exchanging the shame of a Cross for a Crown,
He triumphed o'er death!
The women who wept at the tomb in their sorrow;
The angels, disciples, all joyfully say -
The Lamb who was slain, is King of all ages:
He gives victory and blessing to all who obey:
Then let us remember the will of our Father,
And gladly press on.

Obedience and Blessing

READING   Jeremiah 22: 1-17 and 23: 1-4

'Thus says the Lord: "Execute judgement and righteousness, and deliver the
plundered out of the hand of the oppressor. Do no wrong and do no violence to the
stranger, the fatherless, or the widow, nor shed innocent blood in this place.
'For if you indeed do this thing, then shall enter the gates
of this house...kings who sit on the throne of David.'   *Jeremiah 22: 3 & 4*

*H*istory records the triumphs of those nations that obeyed this truth. Britain has only to look at the reign of Queen Victoria to be reminded that the secret of her success was the Bible. History also records the triumphs of the Gospel, when Ireland became known as, 'The Land of Saints and Scholars'. Prior to the advent of Saint Patrick, under the Druids, Ireland was totally pagan - they had no concept of the only true God and His Son Jesus Christ. P.W. Joyce in his 'Concise History of Ireland', records - 'Many worshipped idols of some kind: some worshipped water. They were skilled in magic - indeed they figure more conspicuously as magicians than in any other capacity - were believed to be possessed of tremendous preternatural powers. They practised divination, foretold future events from dreams and visions - from sneezing and casting lots, from the croaking of ravens and the chirping of wrens. They bitterly opposed Christianity - and we know that there were Druids in the country long after St. Patrick's time, who continued to exercise powerful influence.' Joyce goes on to elaborate on their belief in fairies ('Shee') "who were worshipped by the Irish, as local deities who were supposed to live in the interior of pleasant green hills or under great rocks or sepulchral cairns, where they had splendid palaces.' (Many of the Fairy Hills are still known all over the country).

It was to this Ireland that St Patrick came with the message of the Bible, and Ireland rose from paganism to be an influence for good throughout the world. Sadly, today it is the opposite. I had the privilege of surgery and treatment in the British Hospital in Buenos Aires. I am so grateful for the love, attention and kindness shown to me and have happy memories of doctors and nurses and friends I made while a patient! But my only sad memory during my stay was chatting to a man from the West of Ireland. (Probably his ancestors had gone to Argentina when the British planted the railways there). In conversation, he asked me if I had listened to the news that morning about "rioting in Belfast". When I replied in the negative, he told me what had happened and challenged me with the need for missionaries in Ireland!

Argentina has suffered since that time, but today, despite the economic crisis and other national concerns, God is moving by His Spirit. I was delighted to know of thousands of Argentinians, including some government officials, gathering on what must be the widest street in the world, Avenida 25 de Mayo, for prayer for their country. Thousands have professed faith in Christ and there is hope for a more prosperous future. Oh that we might see God move in our nation and throughout Ireland, - North and South!

Have we failed to reach our "Jerusalem and Judea"? We have sent many missionaries to various parts of the world, but perhaps we have neglected our nearest 'Mission Field'! Let us ask for God's forgiveness and repent of our sin of failing to obey 'The Great Commission' and, as the body of Christ rise to the need on our doorstep - taking the love of Christ to the lost!

The Call

"I need you," still the Saviour calls,
"to serve Me day by day,
so at My bidding, take this news -
I died sin's price to pay.

It may not be in a foreign land
your service I require
to speak to those who've never heard -
help lift them from the mire!

Your gifts and talents I will use,
My life through you I'll pour:
Your heart of stone I'll take away -
I'll melt you more and more.

Then life will be, in service free,
A living sacrifice!
A vessel, holy unto Me -
whate'er may be the price.

When in eternity you stand
and meet Me face to face -
how glad you'll be that you agreed
 to run a noble race."

Perplexed Yet Not in Despair

READING   2 Corinthians 9

'We are hard pressed on every side, yet not crushed; we are perplexed,
but not in despair... struck down, but not destroyed.'   *2 Corinthians 4: 8, 9*

Watchman Nee wrote, 'From the first day I was converted, my sincere ambition was to be a true Christian. Of course I had my own conception of that kind of Christian. A true Christian, I reasoned, should smile from morning to night! If ever he shed a tear, he had ceased to be victorious. He must, too, be unfailingly courageous. The slightest sign of fear would mean he had failed seriously to trust his Lord. He had, in fact, fallen far short of my standard. 'But the Christian life, I soon learned, is very different. It is a paradox of power in weakness, joy amid pain, faith triumphing in the presence of doubt. When the Christian is strongest in the Lord he is often most conscious of inability; when he is most courageous he may be profoundly aware of fear within; and when he is most joyful a sense of distress readily breaks upon him again. It is only 'the exceeding greatness of the power that lifts him on high'.

Are you perplexed or in despair today? You are not alone. Many of God's people are experiencing hardship and feel discouraged, just like you. Some are battling with doubts and wonder if God is still interested in them. Perhaps your problem is that you have failed your Lord and wonder if there is forgiveness for you. The Bible clearly exhorts us to repent and turn again to the Lord asking for His pardon. 'If we confess our sins, He is faithful and just to forgive us our sins and to cleanse us from all unrighteousness'. *1 John 1: 9.*

Whatever we have done God will forgive us, for His mercy and grace is extended towards us continually. The only pre-requisite is genuine repentance - it means a round about turn, leaving sin and going in the opposite direction with a sincere determination not to return to one's sinful ways. That is the only forgiveness that is genuine! Do you feel forsaken? Are you cast down? Again you are not alone. Thousands feel the same today. Come to the Saviour and cast yourself on His unfailing love. He will never forsake you. 'God is your refuge and strength, a very present help in trouble. Therefore, we will not fear, though the earth be removed and the mountains be carried into the sea'. *Psalm 46: 1,2.*

The worst scenario is that the mountains be removed - or the end of our civilisation, as we know it. God says through the Psalm that even this were to happen, He is still our refuge and help - He cannot fail for He is God! His promise can be trusted, so be encouraged, you are not forsaken. Lift your eyes to the hills, gaze on the dying form of the Son of God and remember that **He died for you** and has sent His Holy Spirit to abide in you. You are not alone. Trust Him!

Not Rejected

Not rejected -
   The prayer of my heart;
When to God I drew near
With my turmoil and fear;
He heard my faint cry,
As to me He drew nigh:
Not rejected -
   God answered my sigh.

Not rejected -
   That longing for peace;
When my heart sighed for rest
And to be at my best;
He came like the dove
Bringing comfort and love:
Not rejected -
   In Heaven above.

Not rejected -
   My yearning to serve;
When I yielded my all
And I answered His call;
My joy was complete
As I fell at His feet:
Not rejected -
   At the Mercy Seat.

Remembering God

READING   Ecclesiastes 12

'Remember now your Creator in the days of your youth...'   *Ecclesiastes 12: 1*

*L*ife is a journey from the cradle to the grave and every milestone is significant in our development. Childhood is such a happy, carefree season, when we discover, explore and just enjoy the pleasure of living without any responsibilities. All too soon these years pass and we emerge into our teens with all its physical and physiological changes shaking our confidence, while at the same time producing a sense of independence. Youth is the time of mental development and agility. No doubt, it is because of this that we are exhorted to 'remember our Creator'. It is significant that most people come to faith in Jesus Christ in childhood and early in their teens. The prophet gives us the reasons for such an exhortation. The twilight of life comes when failing health saps the pleasures of youth. - He mentions failing eyesight, no pleasure in youthful pursuits, men losing strength because of weakening bones - even few dentures left to do the job for which God intended; fears of heights and dangers that previously did not give cause for concern.

The prophet concludes his poem -

'For man goes to his eternal home, and mourners go about the streets.
Remember your Creator before the silver cord is loosed.
Or the golden bowl is broken,
Or the pitcher shattered at the fountain
Or the wheel broken at the well
Then the dust will return to the earth as it was,
And the spirit will return to God who gave it.'

Whatever stage in life you have reached, the important question is - Have you remembered your Creator, remembered His plan of salvation, repented of sin and found 'peace through the Blood of His Cross? Having received Christ as your Saviour, have you remembered to spend time with Him today?

Crossing Life's Bridges

Love is the bridge over which you begin
life in a world that is tarnished by sin;
Many the bridges you'll then have to cross
- some will bring gain and some will bring loss.

Learning is the bridge over which you will go
to pastures of knowledge in order to know
a pathway fulfilling and a life that's worthwhile
- setting up goals at the very last mile.

Salvation is the bridge God provided for all
who will turn from their sin and answer His call;
By repenting and seeking forgiveness, you'll find
God will give pardon and real peace of mind.

Death is the last bridge over which you will tread
and providing you're ready, you've nothing to dread
- your spirit will quietly cross to God's Home,
so don't be afraid when you hear Him say 'come'!

How to Deal With Fear

READING   John 20: 19-31

'Then, the same day at evening, being the first day
of the week, when the doors were shut where the disciples
were assembled, for fear of the Jews, Jesus came and stood
in the midst, and said to them, "Peace be with you".'   *John 20: 19*

One can picture eleven frightened disciples gathered together in a room with the doors shut. They were scared stiff! After all, their leader had been crucified and the Jewish leaders were keeping a close watch to see how the followers would react. The previous days had been tense. Peter had denied his Lord and the others were silenced in fear. It was this fear that drove them to hide behind locked doors. It was a natural reaction - they had barricaded themselves in a room and locked the doors. Imagine their surprise when Jesus stood in their midst and spoke to them! His words must have been like healing salve on a wound - 'Peace be with you'. One can almost feel the tension lifting from their tired stressed bodies and minds and a feeling of relaxation entering into their entire being.

Have you ever sensed such fear? It may be fear of those in authority over you or fear of a situation that could have serious results. It may be fear of a terminal illness or fear of losing someone very dear to you, fear for your children's future - whether for their career or for their health. No doubt, in some way, you can relate to the fear of those disciples. Have you reached a situation where you fear you will 'cave in'? In verse twenty we read, 'Then the disciples were glad when they saw the Lord'. My friend, if you are afraid today, just recognise the presence of the risen Lord. He has said, 'I will never leave you nor forsake you'. He has not changed and can come and fill your frightened mind with His peace until you sense release from the tension caused by fear. It was the presence of the risen Saviour that dispelled the fear of the disciples. 'It is always darkest before the dawn' and 'every cloud has a silver lining' are worthy sayings, so look up and put your trust in the Living God, who never fails to keep His promise. Whatever the difficulty, whatever the problem, there is nothing too hard for our God. We worship and serve the God of the impossible! The situation the disciples found themselves in was an opportunity for the impossible and subsequent events proved this to be true.

Jesus breathed on them and they were filled with the Holy Ghost as He commissioned them to go and preach forgiveness of sins. Did the Jews attitude change towards them? No! Of course not! The Jews still hated them and, if it had been possible, would have put more of them to death. History records that many did ultimately die for their faith. The situation around them did not change - the change was the attitude of the disciples to persecution and possible death. They became fearless! They were given such courage, strength and vision, that physical suffering and persecution was unimportant. They had a mission and nothing would stop them in fulfilling that mission. The big difference was that they had the risen Christ with them. Jesus would leave them but He gave them the Comforter - the Holy Spirit. Dear friend, the antidote of fear is to have the presence of the Holy Spirit in your life. Receive Him by faith. When you do this, fear will leave you and you will be strengthened and given courage to face impossible situations.

If you believe

'All things are possible to those who believe'
said Jesus to men in distress:
they knew the Saviour was going away
and they felt that their cause would be lost:
Would He not establish a Kingdom on earth,
Bring peace to a troubled world?
What did this mean for the group of men
Who followed the lone Nazarene?

'Did I not say that if you believe
- you would see the glory of God',
These were the words that Jesus said
to Martha when Lazarus died:
She felt the Saviour was not aware
of the grief she hid in her heart
and through her tears she cried in despair
- to the Healer of Broken Hearts.

Now we can see the purpose of God -
to forgive a fallen race.
Despite the fear and frailty of man,
God began the era of Grace:
He had a plan far greater than theirs
- to bring peace to a troubled world
and herald the message of 'sins forgiven',
through the blood of His Cross.

Pause and thank God for His wonderful plan of Salvation!

135

Exercising Self-control

READING   Proverbs 25: 28

'Whoever has no rule over his own spirit,
is like a city broken down, without walls.'   Proverbs 25: 28

*T*he mind is a battleground. Daily we are attacked through eye-gate and ear-gate, so we must be on our guard to have the Lord as our protective shield - like Abraham and the apostle Paul, taking faith for a shield to quench the fiery darts of the wicked one. In ancient civilizations, the primary defence for cities was huge imposing walls. When the walls were surmounted, it meant victory for the aggressor. Solomon likens a person without self-control to a conquered city. When self control is gone, one is at the mercy of external forces. The enemy has conquered the seat of power and turbulent emotions and passions are in total confusion. 'Double-minded' was how the apostle Paul describes this inner turmoil. It is not by exercising more self-determination that we maintain, or regain self-control: not doubling of one's efforts or even in better time management. The pivotal discipline for godly self-control is the renewing of the mind. Like the ancient walls of a city, the mind is the crucial defence mechanism and bombarded with negative, critical, undisciplined, evil thoughts, the behavioural pattern and the entire personality of the individual are adversely affected. How then can we amend our ways? The first step is to understand our position in Christ, and that depends on our relationship with Him. We must recognize that we have been crucified with Him - '...reckon yourselves to be dead indeed to sin... Romans 6:11a

We are buried with Him and raised with Him. Now 'we are seated with Him in heavenly places...'. He is living on the inside by His Holy Spirit - Godly self-control can only be achieved as His power renews our mind. The outworking of this daily renewal directs and controls our actions. Guided by the power of the Holy Spirit, we balance poise and spontaneity. Naturally our habits and ability to exercise self-control are formed by the influences of the home, our social environment and education. The scriptures teach us that Christians are 'under new management'. Paul exhorts believers to '... present your bodies a living sacrifice...' - that includes the will and the mind as well as all the other members of the body. It is only when we make Jesus Christ 'Lord of all' that we come under the control of the Holy Spirit. Then life in the Spirit becomes supernaturally natural and our habits and ability to exercise self-control is not a struggle but a delight.

'Take my will and make it Thine
It shall be no longer mine:
Take my love, my Lord I pour
At Thy feet its treasure store.'

To be like Jesus

LORD HELP ME
To be the person You want me to be:
To see the needs You want me to see:
To do the things You want me to do:
To love the people You want me to love...

UNTIL
I am the person You want me to be:
I see the needs You want me to see:
I do the things You want me to do:
I love the people You want me to love.
Amen!

The Mountain of Recovery

READING   Isaiah 61: 1-11

'...that they may be called trees of righteousness,
the planting of the Lord, that He might be glorified.'   *Isaiah 61: 3b*

Life is a series of plains, valleys and mountains. At times we can travel along a flat uneventful plain, which brings a sense of contentment, security and a feeling of wellbeing with no highs and lows. This is enjoyable but if all of life were lived on the plain it would become monotonous. God's pattern for living involves the plains, but thankfully it has variety and we all have experienced the valleys and mountains as well as the flat restful plains.

The first three verses of Isaiah bring us through valleys and mountains. There are valleys of poverty; a broken heart; captivity and prison; the vengeance of God; mourning and the spirit of heaviness. Then Isaiah moves on to the mountains of good tidings; liberty; freedom; comfort; beauty; joy, and praise. The verses climax with the assurance of 'beauty for ashes, the oil of joy for mourning, the garment of praise for the spirit of heaviness' for the purpose of producing righteousness. There are times that we can prolong the valleys when God wants us to climb the mountains and soar to heights of new experience and blessing. For example, if we were to dwell too long in the valley of mourning, it would become too painful and our grief could become unbearable. Thus Isaiah exhorts us to bring a message of hope and of adorning one's self with the garment of praise instead of the spirit of heaviness and to take the oil of joy for mourning. It does not disrespect the deceased but gives us hope for the future. God may be saying to you today - 'I want to bring you from the valley of mourning to the mountain of a new beginning - give Me your sorrow and tears! I understand your heartache and grief, leave your loved one with Me and face life with My garments of praise. Go forward into the future to see what My plan is for your life'.

Make this day a new beginning and start to climb the mountain of recovery so that you may prove what is that good and acceptable and perfect will of God'.

Let go of your grief and let God give you His comfort.

Garments of Praise

No disrespect for widowhood
nor disregard for pain
I laid aside my heavy cloak
for I must live again;
I clasped the hand of courage
let go of doubt and fear:
I swept out all the ashes
so beauty could appear
God says the night of sorrow
will vanish with the dawn
so why should I be weeping -
when He offers me A SONG!

A Refuge in the Storm

READING   Judges 20

'God is our refuge and strength, a very present help in trouble...'   Psalm 46: 1

*I*f you have ever watched the birds at the Cliffs of Moher or a similar rugged coastline on a stormy day, you will have seen the gulls, puffins and a variety of birds securely nesting in the rocks. Their feathers are not ruffled, nor are they anxiously looking around for danger - No! Some of them may even have their eyes closed! They are totally relaxed because they have found a refuge in the high rocks and will shelter until the danger is past. In the same way, God comes to His children in the storms of life and invites us to take refuge in Him.

In Judges chapter twenty we read of God's provision for the Children of Israel. God told Joshua to speak to the people and tell them to appoint cities of refuge for the protection of those who accidentally or unintentionally had killed another person. Those who would flee to the entrance of one of the cities of refuge and declare their case in the hearing of the elders, would be taken by the elders into the security of the city. Then when the avenger of blood pursued him, the elders would not deliver him to their hands - He was safe! Those who have fled to Christ and taken refuge in Him as Saviour and Lord have found a tried and safe refuge. It is the most secure refuge known to man for it is the Eternal God. 'The eternal God is your refuge and underneath are the everlasting arms.' **Deuteronomy 33: 27**. Whether the gale that has hit your life is something that will pass or life threatening, God wants you to take shelter in Him.

During the last war when fighting was fierce on the Normandy beaches, a crowd of young soldiers came off duty to find refuge in one of the huts provided by the Christian Soldiers' Association. They were cold and wet after hours in the trenches. Some relaxed over a hot cup of freshly brewed tea, others secured a spot to read and some wrote letters home. Suddenly above the din there were three short, sharp blasts of the sentry's whistle, the signal for 'lights out'. Then, almost immediately, there was the distant whirr of enemy aircraft. In a moment the hut was cleared - all but a dozen young Christians, who remained where they were. One of the soldiers was seated at the piano when they were plunged into darkness. Bombs dropped in quick succession! The young pianist's hands trembled over the keys, and, in the words of John Wesley's hymn, he prayed as he softly sang...

'Other refuge, have I none,
Hangs my helpless soul on Thee:
Leave - ah leave me not alone,
Still support and comfort me:
All my trust on Thee is stayed,
All my help from Thee I bring:
Cover my defenceless head
With the shadow of Thy wing.'

Then the group of Christian soldiers knelt down and asked their Heavenly Father to keep them safe. God wonderfully preserved them while many of their comrades, who had taken refuge elsewhere, were killed - including the nearby sentry, who had sounded the alarm.

Take refuge today in the eternal God - it is the only safe place to be.

Hidden Treasure

READING   Ephesians 2: 14-22

'Again the kingdom of heaven is like treasure hidden
in a field, which a man found and hid; and for joy
over it he goes and sells all that he has and buys that field.   Matthew 13: 44

This is a delightful little parable tucked into one verse in Matthew's gospel. I can imagine this farmer spotting the ground and discovering the hidden treasure. He reasoned that if he sold everything and bought the land, both the land and the treasure would be his. We are not given details of the negotiating, frustrations and difficulties of selling all that he had, but obviously there was a great deal of hard work involved from he discovered the treasure until the field was purchased. Eventually, the day comes when he is the proud owner of this very valuable piece of land. Then he digs for the treasure. Can you imagine his surprise when he discovers he is a wealthy man?

Bible commentators tell us that this would have been common in Bible times and the find would probably have been valuable pieces of jewellery - no doubt protected in a leather bag or several leather bags. One can picture the scene of a very excited and satisfied man pulling one piece of jewellery after another out of the bag! We are told that the treasure was hidden, therefore the man had no idea of its real value, but knew that it was worth having and therefore made the decision to take a financial risk and sell all to buy the field. This is like the new birth. We enter the family of God through taking a step of faith in the atoning work of the Lord Jesus Christ on the cross of Calvary. Then we venture out on the promises of God and discover the gift of pardon, assurance of heaven, joy in believing, peace with God and the peace of God in our hearts and lives. These and a multitude of other blessings are all contained in God's 'hidden treasure'. It is only when we trust Christ as Saviour and Lord that we discover these treasures. What a discovery! Besides the joy of forgiveness from the penalty of sin and peace with God through our Lord Jesus Christ, the discoveries produce harmony in our lives and bring us a purpose for living.

Death will not end our discoveries because -
'Eye has not seen, nor ear heard,
Nor have entered into the heart of man
The things which God has prepared for those who love Him.'

What a prospect! Beyond the valley of the shadow of death, there is a new beginning for the Christian. It will take us forever to discover the things that God has prepared for us.

Death is Gain

When I reach the boundary and step out of time,
the Saviour will be there -
say, 'child you are mine'!
I'll go with Him gladly, for He knows what's best
- He'll take my weak spirit to realms of the blest.

When I reach the Jordan, I know He'll be there
to take me to mansions He went to prepare:
death's valley He'll brighten for He is the Light -
no darkness will linger - It's only 'goodnight'!

When I reach the Glory, how glad I shall be
to waken in heaven and my Saviour see:
the mysteries now hidden, will all be made plain -
as fulfilled are the scriptures - 'to die is gain'!

Simplicity in Prayer

READING   Matthew 6: 5-15

'Our Father in heaven, Hallowed be Your name'.   *Matthew 6: 9*

*T*oday, we consider the simplest, yet most profound prayer of the New Testament, what we rightly call, 'The Lord's Prayer'.

We can understand the disciples feeling inadequate in the realm of praying. They had come from different backgrounds and from a religious faith that depended on another making prayers on their behalf. Now they are discovering that Jesus Christ was opening up a 'new and living way' for them as individuals to approach God. As yet they had not received the full revelation of who Jesus Christ was and of the possibilities of prayer that would be opened up for them after His death and resurrection. But Jesus was training His followers for the time when He would not be present with them and they would have to discover the secret of prevailing prayer, with the aid of the Holy Spirit helping them. It begins with the 'Fatherhood of God' - Our Father! The Old Testament prayer of Jehoshaphat was similar, in that his approach was - 'The God of our Fathers' - also commencing with the 'Fatherhood' of God'. There is no other approach to Almighty God. He is indeed, 'the Father of all mankind' and 'those who come to God must believe that He is and that He rewards those who diligently seek Him'. You may not have had a good relationship with your earthly father and therefore you may find this difficult. Perhaps a good idea is to think of someone you know who has had a really good experience and think of such a father - a father, whose only interest and desire is the good of His child.

Each morning at family prayers, little Tommy prayed for a bicycle for his birthday. As his father listened to that prayer, he knew that Tommy was not ready for a two-wheeled cycle. What would he do? He went to the shop and bought a three-wheeled cycle. Tommy came down to breakfast with expectancy. But when he saw the three wheels, he was disappointed! "I wanted a two-wheeled cycle," he announced! The understanding father explained to Tommy what the dangers of a two-wheeled cycle are and when he would be a little older, he would get one. This is a simple illustration, but one that brings out the fatherhood of God as both loving and caring and 'giving good things to His children'.

The prayer the Lord taught His disciples goes on to focus on where God is - in heaven! This lifts the mind and thought beyond our earthly outlook and into the realm of the spirit and the dwelling place of our Maker.

The next focus is on the 'name' of God. How important this would be when the Son of God would be revealed in His full glory as the 'risen, exalted Son of God' through whose name, is our only approach to God. But the time of revelation was for a later stage. There is no other name through which we can come and in no other name will we have an answer to our prayer.

> *'Take the name of Jesus with you*
> *Child of sorrow and of woe -*
> *It will joy and comfort give you -*
> *Take it then where'er you go!'*

Jesus now moves on to 'petition'. 'Thy kingdom come, Thy will be done on earth, as it is in heaven. Give us this day our daily bread and forgive us our trespasses' ... all prayer should contain the element of petition. Because we are unworthy and dare not approach our God, contrition is the automatic shift of this simple prayer. It is almost in the same breath as petition, that Jesus teaches His disciples the necessity of confession and repentance - in fact the two cannot be separated for no genuine prayer can omit contrition. Then the prayer slides back into supplication for help to avoid sin. It ends by climbing the stairway of praise and worship again. What a triumphant finish! - Jesus concludes His teaching on prayer by affirming that the Kingdom, the power and the glory belong to God forever and ever.

Lord, Teach us to Pray

Teach me the secret of day after day
entering the closet and learning to pray:
Lay Your own burdens on my heart and my mind,
then give me the power - the devil to bind!

145

God's Handwriting

READING   Colossians 2

'Having wiped out the handwriting
of ordinances that was against us...'   *Colossians 2: 14*

As a child I understood that God was keeping an account of my sins and, in my own way, tried to imagine God with a pen writing down all the wrong things I did. I must confess I was a bit sceptical and thought it was just older people trying to scare me into doing what was right. But then one day I read in Colossians chapter two some very alarming words - 'Blotting out the handwriting that was against us, that was contrary to us, and took it out of the way, nailing it to His cross'. I realised that this was a fact, not fiction, as I had thought, and I was frightened. Whether we want to believe it or not, it is true - God, in some mysterious way, has a record of all the sins that you have ever committed. Unless those sins have been repented of and forgiven, one day at the great white throne judgement, He will judge each individual according to what is written in His book. But, because of His mercy, He has made a way of escape. Paul writing in this same chapter says - 'But you, being dead in your sins... He has quickened together with Him, having forgiven you all your trespasses...' We are also assured that when we repent and receive God's forgiveness, our names are recorded in another book - The Lamb's book of Life.

The apostle John had a revelation while a prisoner on the Isle of Patmos. He records - 'I saw the dead, small and great standing before God; and books were opened. And another book was opened, which is the Book of Life. And the dead were judged according to their works, by the things which were written in the books.' *(Revelation 20: 12).* How marvellous that God has provided salvation for the whole of the human race! We do not need to take the punishment for our sins because justice has already been satisfied and the wrath of God appeased - '... the Lord has laid on Him the iniquity of us all' and 'by His stripes we are healed'. Isaiah 53: 5,6.

One day a child of five years spotted the vapour of a jet in the sky, and following with wide-eyed awe, said, "Doesn't God write beautiful?" Whether it is the child in me - or the poetic bent, I do not know, but on many occasions the vapour trail of a jet has had a profound effect on me. I have never seen two sets of vapour trails alike. On a clear day I have noted the sharpness of the trails immediately after the jet passes overhead, then watched them fade - but as I have kept my eyes on the fading effects of the trails, I seem to retain their outline even when the sky has cleared! On a cloudy day, it is fascinating to watch the trails appear and disappear behind the clouds - This reminds me of playing the game of 'hide-and-seek' when I was a child! One could draw parallels with many of the experiences of life from such sightings, but the words of the young child give food for thought. If only we could capture the images of such phenomena, and appreciate their beauty, life would certainly become more colourful!

Friend, God has written in beautiful letters the promise of forgiveness. Have you received it?

God's Answer

Can someone tell me how to find
Release from guilt and peace of mind,
Forgiveness from the sins of years,
Deliverance from my doubts and fears?
Please tell me slowly lest I miss
The pathway to eternal bliss;
Use language I can understand,
So I can reach Emmanuel's land.

All we, like sheep, have gone astray,
Each one has turned to his own way;
There is none righteous, no not one,
That's why God sent His only Son
To die upon a Cross of shame,
Take all the punishment and blame
For sinners such as you and me
And die to bring us liberty.

You must repent of all known sin,
Receive, by faith, and enter in;
Then on the merits of His Son
God welcomes home the wandering one,
He listens to the sinner's plea
Through Christ Who suffered on the tree,
For only He can mediate
Who died to open heaven's gate.

When you accept God's gift of love
The Spirit comes just like a dove;
He gently brings His healing balm,
Abates the storm and brings a calm,
To tortured conscience He speaks peace,
The prisoned spirit finds release.
On wings of prayer to God he soars -
With joy he worships and adores!

Special...How Special?

READING   Deuteronomy 10: 12-22

'...the Lord delighted only in your fathers,
to love them; and He chose their descendants
after them, you above all peoples, as it is this day.'   *Deuteronomy 10:15*

We cannot explain God's reason for choosing Israel. But we do know that the founder of the nation was 'a man of God'. Abraham was the chosen one and he proved his commitment to God by his faith. 'Abraham believed God and it was accounted unto him for righteousness', was God's verdict on this great man. He proved his obedience by leaving Ur of the Chaldees and setting off, 'not knowing whether...' All Abraham knew was that he had been called of God and he must obey God, rather than man, whatever the cost. Abraham's other big plus for being so special was that - 'He was the friend of God'.

In the seed of Isaac and Jacob God's favour continued. It is in Jacob, we see God's special favour extended towards this race. When Jacob, who was a deceiver and the most unlikely man on whom a Holy God would set His favour, met with God and wrestled all night, God changed His name to Israel and thus the nation was born. Tracing the history of Israel brings a greater surprise, but also an amazing revelation. Ruth who was a non-Jew and David, who sinned grievously in the sight of God, were chosen to be the ancestors of the Saviour of the world - the Lord Jesus Christ. We cannot explain it, nor can we explain how God, in His mercy, chose to graft in the Gentiles, but we thank Him that He did. Because He loved us and planned to redeem us, we are special. Individually, we cannot explain why some of us have come to a realisation of our sin and need and have repented and been made God's children with all our rich inheritance by faith. But thank God, despite our sin and utter unworthy state, God has reconciled us unto Himself and made us 'heirs with God and joint heirs with Christ'. Whatever happens in this life, we are safe! That's how special we are to God! No wonder we sing - 'I'm so glad I am part of the family of God!'

As God's children, we must take seriously His commands and instructions. Therefore, let us examine these verses in Deuteronomy chapter ten. God says to His special people and to you and me... 'Circumcise your hearts, therefore, and do not be stiff-necked any longer. 'For the Lord your God is God of Gods and Lord of Lords, the great God, mighty and awesome, who shows no partiality and accepts no bribes.'

The closer we look at these words, the more challenging they become. To gain His favour, we cannot give Him anything (even our service). Not even giving to His cause will help our acceptance, for He accepts no bribes. Whatever we do for God and whatever we give to Him is out of gratitude and must never be in order to gain merit and favour with Him. It does not work, because it is in mercy God deals with us.

Pause in His presence today arid give Him thanks for His goodness. Thank Him for selecting you and leading you to repentance and faith. Thank Him for bringing you into His family - for making you His special child. Thank Him for His daily care and guidance.

It is a good thing to give thanks unto the Lord!

I Thank You

Father, I thank you for the way
You walk and talk with me:
Father I thank you for the day
You set my spirit free!
Father, I thank You for Your love
- Unchanged - 'twill always be
in a world that changes rapidly!

Jesus I thank You for Your Name,
It is my only plea:
Jesus I thank You that you wept
In dark Gethsemane:
Jesus I thank You for Your death
On cruel Calvary
- Now a new and living way I see!

Spirit, I thank You that You came
To give me liberty:
Spirit, I thank You that You guide
My steps unerringly:
Spirit, I pray that You will use
My humble testimony
To the One who bore my awful shame!

Comfort in Sorrow

READING   Isaiah 61

'He has sent me...to comfort all who mourn.'   Isaiah 61: 1,2

At first it might seem strange to read, 'It is better to go to the house of mourning than to the house of joy', but on closer examination and from experience, this is absolutely true. Because it is more blessed to give than to receive, there is a feeling of satisfaction in comforting others rather than enjoying one's personal satisfaction. In joy we are experiencing the feelings of pleasure, happiness and personal gratification, while in giving comfort we are expressing deep feelings of grief and imparting strength to others to cope with their personal loss. There is also the fact that there is only one opportunity to give comfort to another in a particular grief, for death is not repeated, while pleasures can be experienced continually. Our world is full of lonely, bleeding hearts longing for a voice to cheer, crying inwardly because the joys of the past are gone forever - the vacant chair a reminder of the finality of death. Gone are the bonds of love and friendship, and instead a vacuum of pain and loneliness. Take from the world the bonds of love and we are left with a society of hatred and violence. Introduce euthanasia and we rob mankind of the opportunity to care for the elderly and terminally ill of all ages. God is the giver of life and He has ordained that natural death and mourning are part of the entirety of the human life span, incorporating all the outgoing love and care from family and friends and the caring services in the community. Every individual has the right to such care and the right to die in dignity, leaving a sense of loss and appreciation of life without human efforts to terminate it.

One of the most remarkable young women I ever knew was Grace Lyons. Her vivacious jovial nature and outgoing personality was attractive and winsome. Growing up in a happy family atmosphere in Ballymote, Co Sligo, Grace Thorpe was a delightful child who was the life and soul of the party. It was always fun to be in her company. A harmless water-fight or a subtle prank and Grace was 'up front'! Her short life was an inspiration to scores of people and more so during the last six years when she suffered the debilitating illness - motor neurone disease. Grace must have made medical history as the youngest person ever to develop the illness and she will go down in memory as a great example of 'triumph over tragedy'.

The diagnosis of Grace's illness was confirmed shortly after her 22nd birthday. At that time she worked as a computer operator in Dublin. When the news was disclosed to her family and friends, they were devastated. She married Richard

Lyons, a veterinary surgeon, from Dungannon. What a wonderful husband and friend Richard proved to be for the few short years they had together. When Grace was eventually confined to a wheel-chair and later to bed, Richard, Grace's mother and sisters and others supported her and gave her the best possible care and love. What a testimony to the grace of God in suffering and tragedy! When Grace died, she left a heritage for those who continue to struggle with the problem of suffering and death. We receive a new insight into giving comfort to others in similar circumstances. Out of a young woman's illness and death, we have been touched to bring comfort to others.

'Safe in the Arms of Jesus...'

Gone Home

Gone Home; now resting calmly
With the loved ones there,
Gone Home! to be with Jesus
'Mid all that's bright and fair.

Gone where no earthy sorrow
Shall ever enter in,
The pain and weariness all passed,
No blight, no grief, no sin.

Gone - just across the river
to yonder heavenly land,
The lamp of love safe guided,
Held by a Father's Hand.

He saw His child was weary,
The tent dismantled lay,
And stooping down so lovingly,
He carried her away.

Author unknown

Why Are You Troubled?

READING   John 14: 1-7

'Let not your heart be troubled...'   *John 14: 1*

'And when you hear of wars and rumours of wars,
do not be troubled; for such things must happen...'   *Mark 13: 7*

*S*o many people seem to be troubled. If it is not about their health, it is about old age, financial worries, family, society and the growing violence and sin around us.   What concerns you today?   Whatever your problem, you do not need to worry unnecessarily. Jesus taught us that it is wrong to worry. He uses the illustration of the LILY. 'Consider the lily, it does not toil or spin...'

Consider the Lily,
So pure and so white,
With stem tall and slender;
Flower dazzling bright!
In sunshine or shadow,
The Lily's arrayed
In more glory than
Solomon ever displayed!

Consider the Lily,
When robbed of your poise,
By external pressures -
The world's bustle and noise!
Remember her glory,
Came not by hard toil,
But just in accepting,
New life from the soil!

Consider the Lily,
She toils not, nor spins;
When grown, her mouth opens
To praise God and sing!
With no trace of worry,
Her potential she'll reach;
While growing and blooming,
A sermon she'll preach!

Despite such exhortation from the Saviour, it is easy to be caught up with the cares of this life and allow the 'bug' of worry to catch us unawares. Let's face the problem of health! The fact that we are out and able to walk about, is a blessing. With the ageing process, come aches and pains, so we can expect that. But we should not take the burdens of our future health and bring them into the present allowing them to get us down. Young people worry about their future - exam results and a career; who will they marry; will they cope with the responsibility of becoming an adult?

In His teaching on the lily, Jesus goes on to say, "...If God so clothes the grass of the field, which today is, and tomorrow is thrown into the oven, will He not much more clothe you, O you of little faith?" *Matthew 6: 30*

For financial worries, God has promised - 'And my God shall supply all your need according to His riches in Glory by Christ Jesus.' Philippians 4: 19.
Parents and Grandparents worry about their offspring. It is time enough to worry when disaster strikes. It brings unnecessary pain to us when we cross our bridges before we come to them. Let's leave it with the Lord and trust Him to look after our children. He will give the grace when the time comes, but not before it. Are you worried about society and the increase of crime? Yes, that would give us cause for concern. But again we cannot change it over-night, and we just have to pray that God will work His great purposes out for our fallen world. So pray and let God deal with the evil in our society. It must be expected that things can only get worse. The Bible makes it clear that our world is heading for disaster, and the present world crisis, makes us realise that 'it's later than we think'! But even in such circumstances, it is not right to worry. Jesus reassures us - 'And you will hear of wars and rumours of wars. See that you are not troubled: for all these things must come to pass...' Matthew 24:6.

Are you worried about earthquakes and famine in the world? The teaching of Jesus is that we are not to worry but He does teach us to be compassionate and help when necessary and possible. Again this is predicted and is the outcome of man's greed and the increasing sin in our world. Remember that God is working His great purposes out and nobody can stop the hands of time. Look up for our redemption draws near! Yes, it is wrong to worry and get 'up tight' about things. God is with you, my friend, and will see you through. This is not just wishful thinking, but a glorious FACT! When is it right to worry? It is never right to worry! The only thing we should be worried about is the **salvation of our souls.**
'What shall it profit a man if he gain the whole world and lose his own soul?

God's answer
"I have been young, and now am old; yet I have not seen the righteous forsaken, nor his descendants begging bread". *Psalm 37:25*

Surely the God who cared for David in old age, will care for us! (It is generally accepted, that David wrote this Psalm when he was old).

Feet Shod for Service

READING   Ephesians 6: 10-24

*'Put on the whole armour of God...' 'Having shod
your feet with the preparation of the gospel of peace.'*   *Ephesians 6: 11, 15*

Coupled with C.T. Studd, founder of Worldwide Evangelisation Crusade, Emma Munn will be remembered for pioneering in the heart of Africa. Emma was a Belfast factory worker in the early part of the twentieth century. She survived the rough and tumble of family life in a humble terrace house near Gallagher's factory and, despite the scorn of godless work mates, Emma maintained a witness for Christ. She prepared herself for missionary service, and headed for Africa with a sense of call and a commitment to a lifetime of dedicated service. On one occasion when she was trekking through rough terrain in Central Africa, she came to a muddy river - she had no option but to wade through it. It was no mean task to wrench her feet from the grasp of the mud after every step, but she managed to get to the other side. A quick glance at her dirty feet before moving on and Emma, in her inimitable way said, 'How beautiful are the feet of those who preach the gospel of peace!'

Fanny Crosby sums up her surrender in her immortal hymn...
>   *'Take my feet and let them be*
>   *Swift and beautiful for Thee.'*

After the death of the Saviour, Peter's feet took him back to the sea and his fishing boat. He had previously given up everything to follow the Lord Jesus Christ. He had denied the Master before a girl in the High Priest's house and, although he had wept bitterly, his feet had taken him in the wrong direction. But those same feet took him out of the boat and back to the feet of Jesus. Peter would never forget his encounter with the risen Saviour on that day. It must have been humbling for the brave fisherman to be asked three times - 'Do you love Me?' But Peter reaffirmed his commitment and went out to prove it was genuine. His feet carried him in the defence of the gospel until death. Life is a one way journey with death as its final destination. There is no second chance. Therefore we are compelled to consider the direction our feet are taking us. Are they swift to go on the errands of the One whose feet were often weary on the dusty roads around Galilee and whose feet were nailed to a Roman cross as He bore the punishment for our sins?

Live to Give

There I will go, where man is hurting deeply,
Help lift a load: give purpose to his day -
till from dead ashes, he will see some beauty.

There I will sit and let the sounds of love's music
creep in his ears: soft stillness, and the night
becomes rich with the chords of sweet harmony.

Then he will go, where man is hurting deeply -
help lift another's load: give purpose to his day
till captured by the strains, he sings again.

Making the Mature Years Count

READING   Psalm 71

'Now also when I am old and gray-headed,
O God do not forsake me,...'   Psalm 71: 18a

*R*obert S. Peterson knew what it was to make both the early years of his life and the mature years of his life count. He wanted to serve God in an underdeveloped country and set about preparing for a life time of service in helping others less fortunate. He and his wife had all their plans made when he was struck down with polio, which meant he was unable to go abroad. Robert then prepared himself for the Christian ministry in the U.S.A. He exercised an extensive counselling ministry for eleven years, but in 1957 it became necessary for him to leave this ministry due to the physical problem resulting from the polio. However, he continued in counselling and helped people who suffered physical pain.

In his counselling ministry, an elderly lady sought his help with her problem of uselessness. She felt that all her useful days were past. Her children had all 'flown the nest' and had their own homes. When they were small, she enjoyed cooking for them, mending their clothes and kissing away their bumps and bruises. Now she felt she was no longer needed and instead of being a blessing, she was a burden. She wondered why God did not take her Home! In helping someone else, Robert Peterson saw that God had still a purpose for his life and like the Psalmist, knew that - 'It is God who arms me with strength and makes my way perfect.' Psalm 18: 32.

There is a tendency as one gets older to feel not needed – the useful years are past! This of course is not true. God has something for each of His children to do until the day He calls us home to heaven. King David went through the same experience and prays,
'Cast me not off in the time of old age: forsake me not when my strength fails.' Obviously David felt that when his physical strength decreased, people would cast him off because he could no longer perform his duty to his nation as a king. He continues his lament in the Psalm, as he dwells on the ageing process...
'Now also I am old and grey-headed. Oh God forsake me not, until I have showed strength unto this generation and Your power to every one that is to come'. David struggled with failing strength and the fact that his work was not completed. He wanted God to leave him on the earth longer to demonstrate His strength so that the generation to come would know His God.

It is possible that, as he looked back on his life, he felt he had been too busy and had failed to take the time to tell all the great things God had done! Neither did he take the time to write historically for the next generation to know the greatness of God. Although he was a gifted poet and had poetically left some record, he was not satisfied. Now he was old and had time but he felt frustrated because of his physical weakness. But David gives his readers hope! He is not going to give in to despair! He reasons with himself and God, and makes a positive decision to make the most of the time left. He determines not to fear, but to trust God for the declining years , as he has done in the past.

'Hope springs eternal in the human breast', becomes a reality. The Collins dictionary defines 'hope' - 'a feeling of desire for something and confidence in the possibility of its fulfillment'. Hope is not a passing desire, but a positive desire, coupled with the determination to 'pull out all the stops' and make sure the dream is realized.

Whatever stage you have reached in life, you can still find fulfillment as a child of God. There is no retirement in the King's Army. You may not be as actively involved as you would like to be, but there are dreams to be fulfilled and areas to be explored in prayer and devotion, and in influencing the rising generation for God and eternity.

Father

A father's hand will never lead
His child in paths of ill.
A father's heart can never leave
His child to doubt His will.
A father's ear will always hear
His children when they pray.
A father's arm will never fail
To be their strength and stay.
A father's voice will welcome him
When wandering days are done.
So if you've travelled far away
Don't hesitate to call
For God, our Father, always waits
To greet the prodigal.
                    Jean Corbett

God's Looking Glass

READING   1 Corinthians 13

'For now we see in a mirror,
dimly, but then face to face…'   *1 Corinthians 13: 12a*

*W*e seldom get the full picture at a casual glance therefore it would be unwise to form an opinion without observing and assimilating the broader picture. The art student will study the detail of a subject, research the background, and try to understand the mind and emotions of the artist, or the writer, before committing pen to paper, will delve into all possible avenues of information to make sure he has all the facts before publishing his work. Preliminary detail will only serve to whet our appetites for more information. The photographer will poise his camera; test the light, background, shadows, position of the sun and many more details, before his final shot.

Thus it is with the Christian! When we receive Christ as Saviour and Lord, it is with a limited concept of all that is involved that we start out on the Christian life, for 'eye has not seen nor ear heard, neither has entered into the heart of man the things that God has prepared for those who love Him'. We only see through a glass darkly, but here and now we can delve into the Word of God, find Gems of Truth for our daily nourishment and get a broader picture. Ultimately, we shall have a glorious revelation of all the mysteries in Christ and we shall be amazed at our ignorance – or perhaps it will be so plain we will not even have to ask any more questions. What a day of rejoicing that will be! Just as we go daily to the mirror before meeting the public, so too we must go daily to God's mirror, the Bible, to see ourselves in need of strength to cope with the demands of the day. If we look at our image at mid-day, we no doubt will get a different image in the mirror – the hair may be ruffled and the countenance somewhat strained. At the end of the day, it would be different again and in need of attention. Thus, in our spiritual life, we need 'daily manna', so that throughout the day, we will have resources to call on in the hour of temptation and frustration. If the Saviour had to use scripture to attack the Devil, how much more do we need to wield the 'sword of the Spirit, which is the word of God' Ephesians 6: 17.
'As it is written…' said Jesus! If we do not hide God's word in our hearts, we will not be able to 'quench the fiery darts of the wicked'. James exhorts us to keep ourselves 'unspotted from the world' James 1: 27 or as J.B. Philips warns – 'Don't let the Devil squeeze you into its mould'!

God sometimes has to re-make the vessel when it becomes marred, and there are times when the testimony of a Christian spoils the witness. Even then, God graciously lifts the broken pieces and gives to His repentant child, a new ministry. His forgiveness is total! 'As far as the east is from the west, so far has He removed our transgressions from us'! Psalm 103: 12.

God is gracious and patient with His children and although we are not the Christians we would like to be, we rejoice that we are not the rebellious sinners we once were!

The Sherd

A potter with painstaking effort,
　　　　fashioned a vessel of worth
for a merchant of fame in the city
　　　　whose clients were known for their wealth:
The vessel was valued and traded,
　　　　then bought by a handsome young groom
as a gift for his dearly beloved
　　　　to adorn their Jerusalem home:
The vessel was that of a pitcher
　　　　once used by women and girls
to draw from the wells of Judea
　　　　water for family and friends:
The groom gave the prized possession
　　　　to his bride on their wedding day
- Said, 'this will remind you of mother
　　　　- now gone, but her memory will stay!'

In the home of this young Jewish couple,
　　　　the pitcher was greatly admired;
Some said it was priceless, a beauty!
　　　　Something that all would desire!
But one day a two year old toddler,
　　　　while Mamma was making a call
in the home of the young Jewish couple -
　　　　took the pitcher and – CRASH – let it fall!
The women were nearly demented
　　　　when the husband came into the house
- but he picked up the two broken pieces,
　　　　then quietly turned to his wife:
'The pitcher the toddler has broken -
　　　　it won't ever be the same,
but take one of these broken pieces
　　　　to treasure in my Mother's name!

Although the *sherd had no beauty,
    it became the vessel most used
in the home of the young Jewish couple -
    Mother's memory would never be moved!

* "sherd/shard": Jewish families used 'Sherds' to carry live coals to kindle a fire, to siphon water from a container and for many other useful purposes.

Finding God's Plan

READING   Romans 12

'I beseech you, therefore, brethren, by the mercies of God that you present your bodies a living sacrifice, holy, acceptable unto God, which is your reasonable service... that you may prove what is that good and acceptable and perfect will of God'.   Romans 12: 1, 2

God has a special plan for our lives. We have been given the gift of life and it is up to us how we spend that gift. We can squander it, we can abuse it, or we can surrender our bodies to God and discover His will for our lives. In his letter to the church in Rome Paul urges the believers to present themselves to God.   Paul knows that this is the pathway to service and reaching life's full potential. Do you sense the pleading note in his writing? One can almost hear a voice saying - 'I plead with you to give your bodies to God as a living sacrifice! Do not offer Him the tail end of your life, but use the productive years to discover the good, acceptable and perfect will of God.' Friends, this is your reasonable service, so please do surrender your will to God.

Footprints

Let me leave footprints in the sands of time
That others may follow and some purpose find!
Help me not cherish some illusive dream
But serve Christ Jesus, the lone Nazarene.

Let me leave footprints in the sands of time
For short is the life span that I can call mine!
Soon I shall leave for realms of the blest -
May others who walk in my footsteps be blessed!

Let me leave footprints in the sands of time
That others will see as a heavenward sign
Guiding to Jesus, God's only Son
Who willingly 'trod the winepress' alone.

A Friend Who Will Never Fail

READING   Luke 1: 26-56

'A man who has friends must himself be friendly,
but there is a friend who sticks closer than a brother.'   Proverbs 18: 24

*Y*ou may have picked up this book feeling lonely, or perhaps you are facing a new situation in life and feel you need a real friend in whom you can confide. The Bible introduces us to some of the most beautiful human friendships, such as the bonds of friendship between Jonathan and David. Jonathan was prepared to risk his life for David when his jealous and angry father wanted to kill his friend.

It is recorded of Abraham that he was the friend of God. What a remarkable friendship between a man and his God! It developed over the one hundred and seventy five years of Abraham's life. Abraham knew God in such a way that he reasoned with Him over the destruction of Sodom. Such was the intimacy between God and Abraham that a conversation took place between them resulting in Lot being saved when God rained fire and brimstone on a sinful city. The friendship lasted until the end of the great Patriarch's life!

Our reading today, gives us the story of a very special friendship between the Virgin Mary and Elisabeth. Dr Luke gives us a detailed account of the visit that Mary made to her cousin.
'Now Mary arose in those days and went into the hill country with haste, to the city of Judah, and entered into the house of Zacharias and greeted Elisabeth.' Luke 1: 39 & 40. It is obvious that this was a memorable visit for both women. Mary would have benefited greatly from being able to share her secret with another woman. The public disgrace of giving birth to a child out of wed-lock would have weighed heavily on Mary's heart as she 'kept these things and pondered them in her heart'. At last she was able to talk to her cousin, Elisabeth. Did Elisabeth's greeting alarm Mary? I don't think so, because she was carrying the fore-runner of the Lord Jesus Christ – John the Baptist. Elisabeth already knew Mary's secret. With a loud voice she exclaimed...
'Blessed are you among women, and blessed is the fruit of your womb!
'But why is this granted to me, that the mother of my Lord should come to me?' In her salutation, Elisabeth confesses the unborn babe as her Lord!
'For indeed, as soon as the voice of your greeting sounded in my ears, the babe leaped in my womb for joy.

'Blessed is she who believed, for there will be a fulfillment of those things which were told her from the Lord.'

It must have been such a relief for Mary as she listened to these words of encouragement! She had kept her secret. Nobody would understand, only Elisabeth and now they were able to share in the mystery of the incarnation. No wonder Mary breaks into what is now known as the Magnificat…

'My soul magnifies the Lord,

'And my spirit has rejoiced in God my Saviour.' It is noteworthy that these two remarkable women confess the Lord Jesus Christ both as Lord and Saviour! Thus God, in His providence, declares before the birth of the Saviour of the world, His deity and proclaims Him as the only Saviour of sinners.

Is He your Saviour? If not, then you can know Him today by repenting of all known sin, acknowledging Him as the only Saviour and receiving Him by faith. Then, you too will know the 'Friend that sticks closer than a brother.' Because of the pace of life intimate and lasting friendships seem to be few for most people. There does not seem to be time to build up relationships and form healthy friendships. The family of God was meant to be a loving, caring church fellowship, but sadly, because we live in a society that has been tarnished by sin, selfishness and greed, relationships become strained and problems arise. Also, because of the moral decline there is suspicion and distrust. We must cultivate a healthy and warm sense of fellowship within our churches. What we need is a spiritual awakening to revive and quicken our hearts to understand and appreciate fellowship!

Friendships

I treasure the friendships I made in my youth –
a pen-friend, a school friend who told me the truth!
Such friends were true soul-mates – their company I treasured
- the joy that they gave me could never be measured!

I treasure the friendships I made in my teens –
together we shared precious thoughts and sweet dreams
of plans and ambitions, of future success
and a genuine longing to aim for the best!

I treasure the friendships I make day by day –
I know many of these are with me to stay
'till the journey of life has come to an end
and I glance back at death when the road starts to bend.

As I pass through the valley of death's chilling tide –
My Best Friend has promised to be at my side!
Death's valley I'll fear not, for He is my Guide –
He'll take me to Glory, with Him to abide!

Take Your Burden to the Lord

READING   John 11: 1-27

*'I am glad for your sakes
that I was not there, that I was not there, that you may believe...'*   John 11: 1-15

*W*hen you first read the story of the death of Lazarus, you might be forgiven for thinking that Jesus did not care about his close friends for He was not there when He was most needed. Martha thought the same – 'Lord, if You had been here, my brother would not have died'. Luke 11:21. He did care and came in His time, which is always right. The Saviour is still the same! There are times when it would seem He delays in alleviating our pain; times when it would seem He is not listening to the cry for help. But He is always there and will come at the right time. Trust Him! Also remember that your friends are praying and they too will come at the right time. It could be some time after a difficult situation, a misunderstanding, or bereavement - just when you are at your lowest ebb, that a friend will phone you or arrive bringing words of encouragement. God does care and sends us help at the right time!

'When you pass through the waters, I will be with you and through the rivers they will not overflow   you...' Isaiah: 43:2.

You will never know the number of people who have prayed for you in difficult circumstances. Because you are part of God's family, others share your hurt. The person may not have known your specific need, but was in touch with God and felt constrained to pray for you. On the other hand, it could have been someone you knew, who drew close to you in your pain and spoke words of comfort that helped you in your time of need. It may not have been an audible prayer, but you felt understood and loved. You seemed to see God's love reflected in a kind action.

> I remember your words when my sad heart ached:
> I remembered you there when I felt I would break
> 'neath the heavy load of sorrow and loss –
> Thank you for helping to carry my cross!

As well as Christian friends praying for you, Jesus prays for you. He said, 'I pray not for the world but for those whom God has given to me out of the world' – that is you and me! In your moment of extreme pain and heartache, the Saviour was praying. He watched the struggle, He saw your pain, He wanted you to turn to Him and waited patiently for you to 'cast your burden on the Lord' and know

His sustaining. But you were slow to respond. You may have felt a family member would see you through, or a close and trusted friend, but He waited until you eventually saw He was there and needed divine help. As you lifted a breaking heart, He came! It was then you felt His presence and knew He was the only One who understood. What a relief when the burden lifted! Has this ever happened to you?

If you are going through a crisis just now, it is important to remind yourself that you are not alone. The fact that you are not aware of Him does not mean He has forsaken you. Perhaps you should just take the time to recognize His presence and let go of the pain and hurt. Imagine you are standing on a hill overlooking the sea: you take a deep breath and inhale the fresh, clean air – as you do so, your lungs expand and you feel a new person. This is what God wants you to do with your difficult situation. Let go and let God come with His comforting balm. Let Him remind you that you are His special child. He is your friend, so place your hand in His nail-pierced hand and let Him take you into the future.

The Hands of Jesus

He takes the ruins of a marred broken life
in hands that were nailed to a cross,
and out of the ashes of shame and remorse
creates a life that is new.

He takes the earth of a vessel that's spoiled
in hands that were outstretched to care,
and out of the dirt of old earthenware
produces a vessel of worth.

Eyes of Understanding

READING   Psalm 36: 1-12

'...that the eyes of your understanding being enlightened:
that you may know what is the hope of His calling...'   *Ephesians 1: 18*

'Familiarity breeds contempt' is the old adage that could be applied to our worship! Hymnology has left us a rich heritage of truth in word and music, but unfortunately the eyes of our understanding are closed when we sing them. Charles Wesley's immortal hymn 'And Can it be that I should Gain', for example, has a wealth of biblical truth.

> *'Long my imprisoned spirit lay,*
> *fast bound in sin and nature's night:*
> *Thine eye diffused a quickening ray,*
> *I woke – the dungeon flamed with light.*
> *My chains fell off, my heart was free,*
> *I rose went forth and followed Thee.'*

A number of years ago, I had the privilege of being in a youth fellowship meeting in the city of Limerick, in the home of one of the church youth leaders. What a thrill to hear them sing and testify to the blessing they had received at a teaching week-end in Donegal with a group from a similar background. Although I had booked in for B&B, I could not leave the group early – It was so refreshing! In fact, it was through James, the lad sitting next to me that I learned about the work in Tipperary, and later became so involved in it! Eventually, I said to my friend – "We shall have to leave and get back to our guest house." We stepped over the limbs of the young people in that crowded room and when we reached the hall, two teenagers were sitting with the overflow on the stairs. I could not help but be attracted by their excitement and enthusiasm. One had been to Donegal and heard Charles Wesley's hymn for the first time. Her enthusiasm was contagious as she read the above verse.

"Wait to hear this verse!" the young teenager said to her friend who had been unable to attend the teaching week-end! When she read – 'My chains fell off, my heart was free...' her friend interrupted!

'That's what has happened to us!' I had to speak to them before leaving and learn more about their new-found faith. That night in the guest house, you can imagine the topic of our conversation!

Are the eyes of our understanding closed, I ask myself?

Please take time to read the first line of the verse and allow God by His Spirit to open the eyes of your understanding – there are precious gems of truth in these lines! The soul that has not been awakened by the Holy Spirit to the God of Creation through His Son, the Lord Jesus Christ, is imprisoned in the chains of sin and 'nature's night'.

Between 1838 and 1877, George Wade Robinson wrote some of the most beautiful words ever penned which have been treasured by Christians ever since…

> *'Heaven above is softer blue,*
> *Earth around is sweeter green:*
> *Something lives in every hew,*
> *Christless eyes have never seen:*
> *Birds with gladder songs o'erflow,*
> *Flowers with deeper beauties shine,*
> *Since I know, as now I know,*
> *I am His and He is mine.*

In our reading today, the sweet singer of Israel focuses our attention on the blindness and darkness of those who walk in 'nature's night', but also highlights the 'mercy of God' (verse 5). After describing the state of the Godless, (verses 1-4), David, reminds us of 'the mercy, the faithfulness, the righteousness and the judgments of God' and crescendos with the words - 'How precious is Your loving-kindness, O God! Therefore the children of men put their trust under the shadow of Your wings.' He ends the Psalm with a prayer entreating God to continue His loving kindness to those who know Him…' (Verses: 10 & 12).

A Prayer for Spiritual Understanding

Open the eyes of my mind, O Lord
To make my calling sure:
Open the eyes of my heart, O Lord –
Please cleanse me and make me pure!

Born to Die

READING   John 12: 24

'Most assuredly, I say to you, unless a grain of wheat falls into the ground and dies, it remains alone; but if it dies, it produces much grain.'   John 12: 24

A Brazil nut can teach us many object lessons. It may surprise some to learn that the nut we purchase in the shops does not fall from the tree in the size or form which we buy. In fact, the large Brazil nut that falls from the trees in the Rain Forest of Brazil, is about the size of a grapefruit, and is round. Inside this large nut, are two rows of the hard segment nuts that we buy and enjoy cracking open to munch – thoroughly relishing its unique flavour! In order for this large nut to be reproduced, it has to die. All over the Brazilian forest, this happens. Many nuts are gathered and exported across the world, but many fall and take root in the luscious soil of the Brazilian rain forest.

When a man or woman dies on the battlefield, we call it 'The Ultimate Sacrifice'. Why? A life was laid down in order that others might live. Jesus Christ made the "Ultimate Sacrifice" and was God's perfect, priceless 'Corn of Wheat' that died and was buried. But that 'Corn of Wheat' rose from the grave and triumphed over sin and death to 'ever live to make intercession for us'! History has proved that He did not die in vain. He died alone but, because of His atoning death, He is the first fruits of the great multitude that no man can number that will rise to meet Him on the Resurrection Morning and go to be with Him forever. What a hope! What a prospect!
'Greater love has no man than this that a man lays down his life for his friends'. In the light of such love, we can only exclaim – Thank You Lord Jesus for dying for me!

One of the most beautiful stories ever told is the story behind the famous painting "PRAYING HANDS". Two young men wanted to study medicine but neither could afford to do so. They agreed that one of the two would go first and the other would work in order to provide the finance for his friend to study. Then the second young man would go and work as a qualified medical doctor, to provide the finance for his friend. Sadly, when the first one had finished his studies and qualified, the second one had worked so hard with his hands that they were deformed and he could not longer use them and qualify as a doctor. One sacrificed in order that the other could succeed. What love!

Peter said, 'If I have to die with You, I will not deny You...' (Mark 14: 31), but when the hour of testing came, he failed. God was gracious and gave him the opportunity to repent! In His mercy, God often makes our failures a stepping stone to a successful future. The Brazil nut gives us another example of this – A Brazil nut falls to the ground! Someone finds the big nut before it disintegrates in mother earth. He takes it home and skilfully carves a useful souvenir for someone to treasure as a reminder of a visit to the Brazilian jungle (On my desk is a beautiful pen holder, carved by a skilful craftsman from one of the large Brazil nuts). God does this for His children for we read in Jeremiah 19, 'the vessel was marred in the hand of the Potter and He took it and made another vessel, as it seemed good for the Potter to make'.

Let us be those who will place our lives in the hands of the Master Potter, die to self and sin, and 'live unto Christ'!

He Knows

Blessed be God, He knows my name!
In all earth's millions not one the same.
He knows the good and the evil too,
The thoughts I think, the things I do –
Blessed be God He knows my name!

Blessed be God He knows my frame!
He bears its weaknesses and feels its pain.
He sees a heart that longs to serve,
He made each muscle and cell and nerve.
Blessed be God He knows my frame!

Blessed be God He knows my way!
Each twist in the road, till the break of day
He maps each mile that is still to come
And promises strength and a welcome Home –
Blessed be God He knows my way!

Jean Corbett

Gaining
'A Heart of Wisdom'

READING   Psalm 90

'So teach us to number our days,
That we may gain a heart of wisdom'.   Psalm 90: 12

*N*ot all learned men have wisdom. Knowledge put to proper use, can be beneficial but does not produce 'a heart of wisdom'. In fact the advent of modern technology has sometimes produced the opposite.

What then is the secret of a wise heart? In verse twelve of this Psalm, David lets us into the secret. The wise man realises that life passes very quickly and nobody has a second chance. In the light of this truth, David asks God to help him to 'number his days' in order to make the most of the use of time.

Moses is an outstanding example of a man in leadership who gained 'a heart of wisdom'. He needed it for the enormous task of leading the Children of Israel from Egypt to the Promised Land. One of our twentieth century leaders has referred to Moses as 'the greatest leader of all time!' Moses had an inner strength that was supernatural. He could never have led the children of Israel out of Egypt and into their inheritance in his own strength - they would have been victims of their enemies before they left! Moses did not have a body of advisers , or a government behind him. His daily dependence was on his God! He was not proud, but was 'the meekest man on earth'. In one situation, we are told that he took advice from his father-in-law, Jethro, but otherwise he was led personally by God.

What was the secret of his wisdom and strength?
The best way to discover the secret of a man's power is to look at his prayer life - prayers are the expression of a man's heart and thoughts. 'It is not in man to direct his steps' is a spiritual principle that cannot be ignored. There can never be progress and the development of 'a heart of wisdom' without the acceptance and reality of the sustaining hand of Almighty God in His universe. We read, 'Moses enquired of the Lord', and 'The Lord said to Moses' - He had a listening heart! It is not surprising that he made the right decisions for he received his instructions from a powerful God! He prayed and sought God, then acted, thus he was able to lead a large number of people with skill and wisdom.

The author of our Psalm for today was 'a man after God's own heart' and his writings reveal his intimate walk with God, despite his failure. David knew that he could not continue his intimate walk with God and 'gain a heart of wisdom' unless he kept short accounts with God. In Psalm 51 he confesses his sin. He asks God for cleansing and forgiveness and exclaims, 'Then I will teach transgressors Your ways and sinners will be converted unto You.' Psalm 51: 13.

Background and education can be a major factor in 'gaining a heart of wisdom', but very often education and 'know how' in the spiritual realm can be a hindrance. The learned man may feel confident with his education and training and trust his own understanding. Writing to the church at Corinth, the Apostle Paul tells us 'God has chosen the foolish things of the world to put to shame the wise, and God has chosen the weak things of the world to put to shame the things that are mighty; and the base things of the world, and things which are despised God has chosen, and the things which are not, to bring to nothing the things that are, that no flesh should glory in His presence.' 1 Corinthians 1: 27 - 29. God will not give His glory to another and thus He takes Amos, a herdsman, to fulfil His pur poses, or Gladys Alward, who was rejected by organisations to serve as a missionary in China, and uses her to liberate the Chinese children.

David depended solely on God for His success. In the last verse of our Psalm for today, he prays twice - 'establish the work of our hands'. Thus, the secret of David's success as the King in Israel, was in his dependence on God and an awareness of the brevity of life.
'For what is your life? It is even a vapour that appears for a little time and then vanishes away'. James 4: 14b.

The Brevity of Life

Like a bubble on the water
that bursts and disappears -
or vapour from a kettle,
life's span to me appears:
Like flowers in the garden -
they wither, fade and die,
or a rainbow arched so beautiful
that brightens up the sky!
Too soon their beauties vanish -
How short has been their stay!
To the fallen sons of Adam's race,
their life seems just a day!

An Exiles Dream Fulfilled

READING   Nehemiah: 2

'The God of heaven will prosper us,
therefore we will arise and build...'   *Nehemiah 2: 20*

A city once our pride and joy,
the walls in ruins now they lie -
this news made Nehemiah sigh
when told by exile Hanani
in Susa of Babylon:
Nehemiah sat and wept:
A fast before his God he kept!
Of building up the walls, he dreamt -
back in Jerusalem.

Nehemiah's heart was sore -
A burden for his people bore!
'O God of heaven, I implore -
Restore the exiles as before:
Take them back from Babylon!
The sins of Israel I confess -
Hear us in our great distress!
Please give your servant
        'Good Success'!
Give us Jerusalem!

But Nehemiah did not know
how he could leave the king and go
to help his people build and show
the power of God to every foe -
Bring exiles back from Babylon!
One day the king saw he was sad,
when custom was he should be glad!
Would Artaxerxes think him mad
to build Jerusalem?

The prophet was prepared to fight
for exiles who had lost their right!
He told the king about their plight -
'If I've found favour in your sight,
please, let me go from Babylon!'
The noble king assuaged his fears!
When he heard of father' graves
lying derelict for years
in old Jerusalem.

Nehemiah heard God's call
to leave his charge, forsaking all.
he told the king of 'broken walls,
gates burnt' - sights that would appal!
He must go back from Babylon!
The king was quick to make reply -
Letters and help would not deny:
the prophet's goal was drawing nigh -
restore Jerusalem!

Often the work progress was slow!
Often the morale of men was low,
but Nehemiah would not let go -
Jerusalem, the world must know,
would welcome Jews from Babylon!
The leader and the workers toiled -
the enemy was often foiled!
The plan of God would not be spoiled
for his Jerusalem!

When we look back we see the plan,
fulfilled because God saw a man
whom He could trust to
   'claim the land' -
Bring back the weeping exiled band
from the rivers of Babylon!
Fulfilled was Nehemiah's dream -
He died content that he had been
the man to carry out God's scheme -
for new Jerusalem!

Whatever walls are broken down in our society, whatever walls are broken down in our personal lives, let us rise and build! It is easy to pull down walls, but it takes time, skill and hard work to build them. Let us not live in history, but learn from it and build into a stable future.

If the walls of our devotional life have fallen, let us start today to rebuild them. If the problem is sin, come afresh to the Saviour and ask Him for forgiveness and cleansing and start to build into a future that is worthy of the high calling of a Christian.

The apostle Paul concludes his first letter to the church at Thessalonica, with a wonderful salutation and exhortation -

'Now may the God of peace Himself sanctify you completely; and may your whole spirit, soul and body be preserved blameless at the coming of the Lord Jesus Christ.'
Thessalonians 5: 23

Rock of Ages

READING   Ephesians: 2: 1-13

'But now in Christ Jesus you who once were far off
have been brought near by the blood of Christ'.   Ephesians: 2:13

*T*he death of Jesus Christ was the fulfilment of the Old Testament prophecy. From Genesis to Malachi the scriptures point us to the advent of the Saviour of the World through death. Abraham offering up his son on Mount Moriah and God providing a substitute was symbolic of the atoning sacrifice of the Lord Jesus Christ. The plague of 'The Sprinkling of the blood of the lamb on the door lintels' as recorded in the book of Exodus was symbolic of the shedding of the blood of the Saviour on Calvary - 'and without shedding of blood there is no remission'. (Hebrews 9: 22).

While touring in The Mendips in Southern England, I was reminded of a lad who found Jesus Christ when travelling in Ireland. He was going past an old barn where a country preacher was preaching on '...you who sometimes were far off have been brought near by the blood of Christ'. The lad listened and repented of his sin and received Christ as his Saviour and Lord. Later, he became a minister of the gospel. One stormy day he was caught in a thunderstorm in Burrington Combe in The Mendips, about eight miles from Wells, and took refuge between the two massive pillars of rock. It was there in the deep fissure, while sheltering from the storm, that Agustus Montague Toplady was inspired to write the famous hymn, 'Rock of Ages, Cleft for me'. Toplady's hymn has been repeated by generations of sinners, repenting of their sin and seeking God's forgiveness. It has inspired writers and preachers of the Gospel as they have sought to encourage men and women to build on the solid Rock.

One of the Fisk University singers was a survivor of the steamer, 'Seawanhaka' that was destroyed by fire. As the flames spread, he and other fellow passengers flung themselves into sea. Swimming to his drowning wife, he told her to place her hands firmly on his shoulders, while he endeavoured to reach some wreckage. His wife clung to him until she could hold on no longer. Weary and desperate in a bid to save his wife, he encouraged her to "hold on a little longer". Weak in body and mind he mustered all his strength and said, "Let us sing, 'Rock of Ages.' " As the strains floated over the turbulent waters, others raised their heads above the sullen waves and feebly joined in a plea for help...
'Rock of Ages, cleft for me,
Let me hide myself in Thee.'

One after another the shipwrecked survivors received fresh courage to survive. Then in the distance they saw a boat approaching. Could they hold out until it arrived? Many did, and were still gasping the words of Toplady's hymn as they clung to the lifeboats. The singer believes that the singing of the hymn saved many others besides himself and his wife!

A Solid Rock

I have no grounds to come to God -
but on the merits of His blood:
Condemned if on 'my terms' I stand
and try to build on shifting sand!
No, I must build on solid Rock
for thus the teaching of 'God's Book':
and only thus will He accept -
Without the Blood, God will reject!

God Keeps His Promises

READING   Isaiah 9: 6&7 and Luke 2: 8-20

"His name shall be called... 'Prince of Peace...'."   Isaiah 9: 6b

*G*od always keeps His promises! Time elapsed between the prophecy made by Isaiah and the fulfilment of the promise. As we read the history of the Children of Israel, we are aware of the patience of God. He sent prophet after prophet to instruct and warn them, but they continuously disobeyed His commands. Malachi was the last of the Old Testament prophets and he ends his prophecy with a ray of hope -

'But to you who fear My name
The Sun of Righteousness shall arise
With healing in His wings...'   Malachi 4: 2
'Behold, I will send you Elijah the prophet...'   Malachi 4: 5

The four hundred silent years followed, but 'in the fullness of time', God sent His Son to be the Saviour of the world.
We look back on over two thousand years of history and rejoice that God was faithful to His promise. Did the delay mean He had forgotten? History proves the faithfulness of God!

Before the outbreak of the Second World War, Monsieur Frances Meilland, a French rose breeder, walked through his nursery one day. He reached out to rub a particular glossy leaf, and as he did so, the fine serrated edge of the leaf curled slightly over his finger. He knew he had something special! This leaf was unlike anything he had ever grown before - He knew he had a Master Piece! This plant was a treasure and would produce the most exquisite blooms imaginable. He was anxious to experiment, but he had a problem.
The year was 1939, and the threat of war was hovering over Europe. Monsieur Meilland wanted to experiment and develop the rose further and to give it a suitable name, to what he felt would be a winner! His only hope was to preserve the rose.

By June the following year the war had started.
Monsieur Meilland took cuttings from this treasure and then carefully shipped them across the world, knowing they might never leave France.
Four years later he learned that his precious cuttings had left France on the last flight from Paris before the Nazis gained control of the airport! A letter arrived from Pennsylvania, U.S.A. addressed to the distinguished French rose breeder

praising the beauty of his discovery. The rose was ruffled - the petals were cameo ivory and palest cream tipped with a tinge of pink. But the rose had survived!

On the day the city of Berlin fell to the allied and Russian forces in 1945, rose gatherers in California met for a ceremony to name the rose. To honour the occasion, white doves were released into the sapphire sky and Monsieur Meilland's discovery was no longer a secret - The fragile rose had survived the war and was called PEACE!

The Rose

Little red rose, flower of love;
your blush so bright!
your thorns so sharp!
Fair you are in bud and bloom:
You droop with age
but still the perfume of eternal youth
lingers to become
the sigh of memory!

Rose of Sharon, flower of hope!
Face like the sun,
You smile at us;
Under trees and on dry banks
You quickly grow!
With cloak of yellow,
You conquer weeds;
Your blooming becomes
The sign of victory!

The next great event in God's calendar is the Second Coming of the Lord Jesus Christ. Will God keep His promise? Of course He will! His delay does not mean He has forgotten. Certainly, in the light of all that is happening in the Middle East, we must take note! Matthew chapter twenty four is more relevant today than it has ever been in world history. Those scholars, who have given serious thought to recent events in the Middle East, agree that the scene is set for God's intervention in His world. Behind all the events portrayed on the media and through the press, God works silently and mysteriously - He alone knows the moment when 'The Rapture' will take place. One thing is certain, God will keep His promise! Jesus will come! Soon, the Bridegroom will return for His bride. Are we waiting expectantly? Simeon and Anna were ready for the first advent of the Saviour. Are we saying, 'Even so, come Lord Jesus!' Revelation 22: 20.

Apples of Gold

READING   James 3: 1-12

'A word fitly spoken is like apples of gold in settings of silver.'   *Proverbs 25: 11*

*W*ho would not boast of our county in apple blossom time? Tours are conducted and visitors are welcome to view the breath-taking views of the Armagh orchards in spring.

I was born and brought up in the orchard county of Ulster. My grandfather was a fruit grower and exporter. Fruit growing must have been in our genes for all our family maintained a growing interest in the industry. Two of my uncles followed in the family business. Some of the females found the business interesting - my sister was secretary of the Northern Ireland Young Fruit Growers Association for a number of years. Because of this heritage, I am proud of our luscious brambly apples and the delicious eating apples produced locally. I can almost taste the juicy 'Golden Delicious' apples we produce in County Armagh, as I write!

Our text for today sets this 'queen of fruits' in a delightful poetic setting and gives us food for thought for our meditation today.

This proverb conjures up in my mind a scene in County Armagh during the apple harvest season in September. It is unusually hot and the apple pullers are feeling tired - their limbs are aching from climbing trees or bending to pick up 'windfalls', when the ladies arrive with their lunch. Everyone gathers around for the appetizing sausage rolls, savoury sandwiches, served with soup or a cool drink, and a delightful array of Golden Delicious apples tastefully displayed on a wicker tray lined with apple leaves - the under side is turned up to allow the glint of the silver leaf to sparkle through th e apples. The autumn sun lights up the attractive presentation of the fruit of the season. The apples of gold in a setting of silver brings pleasure and is worthy of all the comments of appreciation!

No doubt, you have experienced the pleasure of 'a word fitly spoken'.
It has been carefully chosen to please you and bring a sense of well being. It can sometimes be a word of encouragement that lifts your spirits and somehow becomes the silver lining in your cloud of despair. On the other hand, you may have been hurt by some cruel words that made you recoil into a shell and feel totally mortified.

Have you ever given the Customer Service Official in your local bank, an awkward employee or a difficult neighbour, 'a piece of your mind'? You may have been in the right, but that little member that James warns us about was out of control. You let yourself down and, more importantly, you failed your Lord as His representative to an unbeliever! Perhaps someone has accused you of slander or telling a lie and, because you have been innocent, you have retaliated with venom! It is not easy to accept an injustice, and certainly it can be appropriate to point out the truth to an accuser, but to hit back with the intention of hurting another person is not a Christ-like attitude.

Let us give thought today to that little member of our body which is a powerful weapon for good or evil and ask God to help us control it in difficult circumstances. Just as the delightful array of apples of gold in settings of silver gives pleasure to the apple pullers, so 'words fitly spoken' give pleasure to those who listen.

Just as the delightful array of apples of gold in settings of silver gives pleasure to the apple pullers, so 'words fitly spoken' give pleasure to those who listen.

Sarah was a faithful wife, a good house-keeper and a loving mother. Despite the demands of rearing a large family, she found time to broaden her mind by reading and keeping abreast with current affairs. During the last war, while her husband was fighting for his country, she jotted down her thoughts on paper and, after her death, her family found the following poem...

Advice

Keep your mind from evil
and your tongue from speaking guile;
If we could only do this -
it would be well worth while!

The world would be a happier place
if slanderous tongues were not!
All would be joy and peace
if we, this precious gift had got.

Be thoughtful and kind to those we meet
as through this world we tread;
Look after your friends while they are alive -
not weep for them after they're dead

Speak no evil of your friends
is a lesson for you and me
and we have always something to learn
no matter how learned we be!

But there is one sure armour that will stand
against all form of sin -
It's the grace of Christ our Saviour
and a heart that is pure within!

Sarah McIlveen

Prayer Changes Things

READING   Acts 12: 1-19

'Peter therefore was kept in prison,
but constant prayer was offered to God for him by the church'.   *Acts 12: 5*

*W*hen I worked in Argentina, I had occasion to make a necessary trip from the town of Laguna Blanca in the Province of Formosa to Fontana in the north. The secretary of the mission was visiting and had to be transported to Fontana before returning to Buenos Aires and back to Britain. The trip meant eleven hours on a dirt road. It was the rainy season and I had to find tracks through the hardened mud, hoping it would not rain too heavily and leave us stranded in Mission Tacagle. We did have to stay overnight, due to the bad weather and wait until late afternoon, next day, before starting out again. Eventually we arrived in Fontana and I left my visitor with my colleagues based in a rather primitive church-planting situation.

I knew I had to return to Laguna Blanca to speak at the Sunday services in our church, but the travelling conditions were getting worse. I opted to go via the city of Formosa and stay overnight at the mission base there before setting out on the four hour drive to Laguna Blanca.

It was Thursday. I vividly remember stopping at the River Police base and asking if it was possible to get through to Formosa. They said the road was flooded in three areas but some trucks had managed to get through. When I explained my situation, they said they would not stop me but I risked dangers!

Their advice proved true! I saw the first flooded area looming ahead and accelerated, and charged! Yes, I made it! It was the same at the second flooded area. But when I reached the third, it was too deep and I got stuck in the middle! When I opened the door of my 'Estancera', the water just gushed in around my feet. It was getting late in the afternoon and I knew it would probably be dark before I got help, so I took my torch, climbed out and waded through the water in my sandals. I prayed for guidance as to whether to walk back or forward. I was twenty-four years of age, alone on a stretch of road with not a house in sight. Added to which I was a foreigner! I walked about fifty yards lifting my heart in prayer to God! As I had been concentrating on the bad road, I had not noticed life or houses, but I knew I could walk for miles before I would meet anyone or see a house! I decided my best plan was to go back and wait at the vehicle. Imagine my delight when I turned and saw a truck coming in the distance! Soon my delight turned to shock as I saw the back of the truck loaded with strong, tough Paraguayan men, six or seven of whom were peering over the top of the pick-up truck watching the road ahead. There were also three men in the cab - the driver and two companions. I prayed and asked the Lord for His protection as they stopped and saw my dilemma. God heard my prayer immediately and joking and laughing they all got to work with tow rope and 'elbow grease'! God answered prayer!

The driver of the pick-up truck said
'Turn the key and see if the engine starts'. To the amazement of the men it started. Then the driver said, 'I know you, you are a missionary. I am a Christian too'. They all waved me off and then they drove into the flood, pushing and shoving to the other side and went on their way! By this time it was dark, but I watched them disappear into the night having 'done their good turn for the day'. I too drove off into the night and when I saw the first glimmer of a little house in the forest, I had clocked up thirty- five kilometres!

I got to Formosa and to Laguna Blanca for the services on Sunday!

Yes, God is faithful! He is our Companion and Helper and we can prove His unfailing love when we trust His promises! Prayer changes things!

Does God always answer prayer? Yes, sometimes an instantaneous answer is required and at other times, we may have to wait and watch the providential work of God as He intervenes in response to the prayers offered in His will.

Commissioned

'Son work today,' for am I not thy father,
Who knowest all they gifts, and weakness too?
Is not My call accompanied by enabling
Sufficient for the task I give to do?

'Son work today,' for dreams cannot accomplish
My plans for feeding hungry souls with bread!
Forget thy selfish hopes and aspirations,
And turn thine eyes to Calvary instead.

'Son work today,' for adversaries gather
To enter through the widely open door.
Haste, haste thee then for even while we tarry
The opportunity may pass for evermore.

Jean Corbett

Measuring Spiritual Maturity

READING   Ephesians 4

'And He Himself gave some to be apostles, some prophets some evangelists,
and some pastors and teachers, for equipping of the saints
for the work of ministry, for the edifying of the body of Christ,
'till we all come to the unity of the faith
and of the knowledge of the Son of God, to a perfect man,
to the measure of the stature of the fullness of Christ;'   Ephesians 4: 11 & 13

*G*rowing up spiritually can be painful. James teaches us that to develop patience and endurance there must be trials and testing - that is not something we relish! But we see through Ephesians chapter four that growth is in God's plan for us as individuals and for His church. We should apply our minds to understand how we can best achieve the goal of attaining God's standards.

God was supremely interested in growth for His people from the beginning of time. In Deuteronomy chapter five He exhorts them to fear Him and keep all His commandments always, that it might be well with them, and with their children forever. Obedience is the gateway to spiritual growth and the development of Christian character will have its effect on the next generation, for righteousness is rewarded.

The Lord Jesus reiterated the greatest commandment given to the children of Israel to love the Lord our God with all our heart, soul, mind and strength and our neighbour as ourselves.

Bernard of Clairvaux, mystic, hymn-writer and theologian said, 'We know God only in as far as we love Him'. So we conclude that spiritual maturity comes through obedience to the commands of God and love of God Himself.

Communion with the Lord cannot be separated from spiritual growth - spiritual growth, although the individual is not aware of it, comes as a result of communion with God. The hymn -writer knew something of such growth when he penned those wonderful words -
> *'Oh the pure delight of a single hour*
> *that before Thy throne I spend,*
> *as I kneel in prayer and with Thee my God*
> *I commune as friend with friend?'*

Do we know the joy of such an experience, or has our spiritual life become barren and dry?

Romantics speak of the 'magic going out of a relationship'. Sadly, for a lot of Christians, the 'magic' has gone from their walk with God and they experience the feeling of another well known hymn-writer - William Cowper:

'Where is the blessedness I knew, when first I saw the Lord?
Where is the soul - refreshing view of Jesus and His word?
What peaceful hours I once enjoyed, how sweet their memory still -
But they have left an aching void, the world can never fill.'

Love between two people can be expressed in two ways - by silent communication and understanding of each other where no words or gestures are necessary - this is the result of a deep appreciation, and respect for each other. Secondly, love can be expressed in words and deeds. In the spiritual realm this is worship and adoration coupled with verbal testimony and works that reveal where our loyalties lie. This produces spiritual growth.

When it comes to service, the only motive should be love. We serve Him because love constrains us.

Every true Christian wants to grow, and the only place to grow is at the feet of Jesus. God wants us to grow up and enjoy, not just the 'milk of the word', but also, 'the meat of the word'!

Sacrifice

Take up the cross and follow Christ -
is that a sacrifice?
Be called a fool,
face ridicule -
Is that a sacrifice?
Identify with those who die
to all the world counts gain,
then walk by faith and not by sight
with righteousness the aim -
be pitied by the proud of heart,
thought weak, with no backbone,
or undermined when you've been kind -
Is that a sacrifice?

QUOTE: 'If Jesus Christ be God and died for me, than no sacrifice is too great for me to make for Him.' C.T. Studd.

The Ultimate Sacrifice

READING   Isaiah 53

'He is despised and rejected by men,
A man of sorrows and acquainted with grief.
And we hid as it were, our faces from Him:
He is despised and we did not esteem Him'.   *Isaiah 53: 3*

*A*s we try to take in the predications made by Isaiah, we turn our thoughts to the sombre scene at Golgotha. There are three crosses standing with the three condemned men nailed to them. The crowd below mock while the Roman soldiers carry out their instructions. We picture the last verbal communication between the two criminals on either side of the Saviour - one penitently asking for mercy and the other rejecting Him. Then we try to imagine the final suffering of the Saviour of the World. That cannot be done because, beyond the physical suffering, was the deep inner pain when He was forsaken by His Father as He bore the sin of the world.

Saviour

He was led like a lamb to the slaughter,
a sheep before her shearers was dumb:
Though He was the King of all ages -
Messiah, Redeemer, God's Son,
yet, He was despised and rejected,
He was nailed to an old rugged Cross -
Mocked and scorned like a guilty criminal,
Till it seemed His cause had been lost!

Men stood by the Cross of the Saviour,
they railed on Him shouting, 'Come down!'
But He looked with pity upon them,
before bowing His head to the ground!
What pain and what awful anguish
the Son of God bore on that day,
as He took our sins and our sorrows -
A debt, we could never repay!

Stephen was the first Christian martyr and since that many have been called on to lay down their lives for the Master.

In A.D. 70, under Nero, Christians were tortured for their faith and history has repeated itself until the present day.

I had the privilege of knowing personally one of the heroes of the Congo rebellion.

Ruby Gray from Dromara in Northern Ireland was a lady I highly respected for her devotion to the Lord. She felt God's call to missionary service and was requested to train as a nurse, take a study course at a Bible College and then attend a medical course in London. It took her seven years in preparation before finally arriving in Congo to serve God and the people of Congo. She was a woman who knew God in a very intimate way and would have accepted the possibility of giving her life on foreign soil for the cause of Christ, before leaving her homeland.

After a comparatively short term of missionary service, Ruby was called to make 'the ultimate sacrifice'. The Zimba rebels rounded up God's servant and a number of others and killed them, then threw their bodies into a crocodile infested river. Ruby did not have her family and friends present to pay their last respects, her body was not buried in dignity and there were no flowers placed on her grave, but she has joined the 'unsung heroes' of all generations who will be Christ's 'precious jewels' when He comes to make up His crown!

We acknowledge again the sacrificial death of the Saviour of the world and pause to thank God for the martyrs of the Christian faith who have given everything to obey the last command of the Saviour - 'Go into all the world and preach the gospel to every creature.' Mark 16: 15

'Come Follow!'

They heard the call, 'Come Follow',
   those disciples long ago
and left their occupation -
   the truth of God to know!
Would they be disappointed?
   to make the Christ their goal?
Would they go back tomorrow
   or face with Him the foe?
They heard the call 'Come Follow'
   - those martyrs of the faith

and left their ease and comfort
   - they bravely took their place
among the chosen soldiers
   to fight and die to bring
the Gospel flag to others
   and be loyal to their King
When Jesus comes in power
   to take His chosen Home -
The 'saints' who suffered for their faith
   will be honoured by God's son!

You are Mine

READING   Isaiah 43: 1-21

'Fear not for I have redeemed you,
I have called you by your name; you are mine.'   Isaiah 43: 1

*I*t is impossible to forget that initial encounter with the Lord. You remember the feeling of guilt - you felt as if you were carrying a heavy load and could not lay it down. In John Bunyan's Book, 'Pilgrims' Progress', which is among the great English classics, Bunyan takes this theme and depicts Pilgrim leaving the city of destruction with a burden on his back. As Christian comes up to the Cross, his burden loosened and fell off his back. It tumbled into the sepulchre and he never saw it again. The weary pilgrim has been set free from his burden and he gives three leaps for joy! This of course depicts the sinner repenting of sin and coming to the Cross of Christ, where he lays down the burden and guilt, and the assurance of salvation fills his soul. The Bible tells us that 'there is joy in the presence of the angels of God over one sinner that repents.' Such an experience of God's Salvation brings us into the family of God. We can say, 'I am His and He is mine'!

Not only do we become 'children of God' but we become part of the Body of Christ of which Christ is the Head. In the fellowship of the church we grow together in fellowship. It is not the rapport we experience with an acquaintance we meet on the street and pass the time of day, or someone we occasionally see and update each on personal news. The Oxford Dictionary defines 'fellowship' as, "the state of sharing mutual interests and activities" and as "companionship and friendship". Such fellowship is not static; it is progressive and is developed mutually. Growth in fellowship means leaving one degree of fellowship aiming for a richer and deeper friendship with mutual interests in all aspects of life and living. Real spiritual fellowship can only be experienced by those who are part of God's family. In fact, it is similar to that experienced within a natural family, for we are the family of God.

Our physical body is prone to pains and aches - some have to face more problems than others as far as health is concerned, but at some stage in life, everyone feels pain. So too, in the body of Christ, we face problems and difficulties and the scriptures give us clear teaching on how to cope with such situations. Because we are so linked in fellowship with the entire body, when one member suffers, others are affected - others feel the pain.

You are Mine

To be the Lords when billows hurl their angry blows:
To be the Lords and in life's darkest hour His mercy know
is more than gold or jewel rare -
for this is love beyond compare:
I lay me down in peace content -
no enemy with purpose bent
can thwart the plan of God for me -
For I am His!

To be the Lords, when waters deep the soul destroy -
To be the Lords when every hope is fading fast and cares annoy,
is wealth beyond our dream-
and so when every hope would seem
to be dying like a wounded dove -
God reveals His constant love -
says, 'You are mine'!

Light of the World

READING   Revelation 3: 20 & John 1: 1-12

'Behold I stand at the door and knock.
If any man hears My voice and opens the door,
I will come in to him and dine with him, and he with Me'.   *Revelation 3: 20*

*O*ne of the most remarkable women I ever knew, was a much loved friend and a 'Mother in Israel' - Doris Finlay. I met her when I was a young Christian and she left an indelible mark on my life. I was searching for God in a deeper way and so I sought to glean from the depth of her deep spirituality and knowledge of God.

Her background, as the daughter of a London merchant, meant that she moved in society in the capital and had every opportunity to indulge in the pleasure the city had to offer a young woman. But she had a desire to know God and in His providence she found herself in the nursing profession in one of the large hospitals in London. While on night duty with a young Christian doctor, she discovered he had a personal faith in Christ that was foreign to her. Thus began her search for something that would satisfy the inner vacuum in her soul. One night the doctor quoted - 'Behold, I stand at the door, and knock if any man hears my voice and opens the door, I will come in to him and will sup with him, and he with me'.

The doctor had given Doris a copy of the Scriptures and that night and for several successive nights she read the Bible in her search for the verse, but failed to find it. She concluded the young doctor was wrong and waited until the next time she was on duty with him to tell him. He assured her it was in the Bible and gave her the reference - Revelation 3: 20 - that night she knelt at her bedside and 'opened the door' and invited the Saviour into her life. That moment Doris Finlay began a new life in Christ! Although she did not fully understand the significance of that step of faith, she knew she had found what she had been searching for and went out to discover the 'hidden riches' of walking with her Saviour from day to day. Through reading the Word of God and prayer, she followed her Lord. She was a devoted wife, a faithful mother, a loving and caring grandmother and great-grandmother. Her influence will continue! Like the pebble thrown into the lake - the ripples will go on until they break on the shores of eternity.

The Light of the World

In the book of Revelation,
verse twenty, chapter three;
Here we meet the risen Saviour,
Standing - knocking patiently
outside a door that's bolted,
asking - Oh, so tenderly
for an entrance to the dwelling,
where He can live eternally.
In this masterpiece of beauty,
John depicts for us a scene
of the Saviour's love and pity
and a heart that's closed by sin:
Here we see the Father's mercy
and the patience of His Son -
See that He will gladly enter
open hearts that He has won!
In the list of famous artists,
is the name of Holman Hunt -
If I were asked to rank the paintings,
Hunt's would surely be in front!
Christ outside is standing, knocking
on a door that's bolted fast -
'Light of the World', Your heart
  is breaking
for the one inside is lost!

Hunt was born of simple parents,
when convention ruled the arts:
Realistic! 'Dangerous rebel!'
He was bent to reach men's hearts.
Seeking for a forceful subject
such as Shakespeare or Tennyson,
He was captured by the picture
John depicts of God's dear Son:
Soon the image of the Saviour
in his mind he clearly saw
and with great anticipation
filled his soul with deepest awe!

In an orchard, lit by moonlight,
while the world lay fast asleep,
thus he captured hues most precious -
 *Keble College, Oxford, keep!
Why an orchard, we must ask him,
as we spot the luscious fruit?
Then across the span he whispers,
'Barren soul - just take, and eat!
You have famished in the darkness,
for so long the weeds have grown
high around the door that's bolted -
light outside, you've never known!'

Hunt has captured such expression
of a face that pleads in love:
It conveys Christ's deepest longing
for the heart He wants to move!
Gentle knocking, there's no force used -
such the way God's Spirit moves
in convincing men in darkness -
they the Light will have to choose!
Note the message of the artist
as his picture you admire -
It's the sinner who must answer,
ere the Saviour's patience tire!

This creation on a canvas
of the Saviour of the world,
Brought to fame this humble artist
when the masterpiece was sold.
Now the picture is immortal
and its message is the same -
for the Book of Revelation
makes the truth of God so plain -
Christ is knocking on the heart's door,
bolted fast by years of sin!
Don't you hear His gentle knocking?
Draw the bolt and let Him in!

---

* The original painting now hangs in Keble College, Oxford.

Open to God

READING   1 Samuel 1-28

'Speak, Lord, for your servant hears.'   *1 Samuel 3: 9*

Samuel had been given to God by his mother, even before he was conceived. As Hannah prayed in the temple the Lord spoke to her and with tear stained cheek, she promised her child to the Lord. It was in obedience to that vow, that Hannah gave young Samuel to serve Eli in the temple.

The background is one of Israel's failure and sin. Even the sons of Eli were living in sin and there seemed no hope, for God's chosen people. But into the situation, God places His hand on a youth with a tender conscience - at the time of God's call, Samuel did not know the Lord and the word of God was unintelligible to him, yet God spoke to him and called him. Whether it was an audible voice, a dream or a vision, it is not important - the most important point to note, is that God had His man (in this case a child) to do His work.

There are lessons to be learned from this beautiful story. First of all, there is 'The Samuel Ear'. Listening is something that has become a 'lost art' in this age of 'Hi-Tech', and vocal expression.

I was in the USA in 1996, and went to have my hair cut and blow dried in a hair dressing salon in Kentucky. The girl was very efficient and quite talkative. We had a two sided animated conversation for a while, but I ran out of steam! The silence that followed was welcome, while I mused with my own thoughts. Then after a couple of minutes, she interjected, in her excited Kentucky drawling dialect - `Talk! Talk!' I was somewhat taken aback and replied, 'What do you want me to say?'

'I don't care', just talk!' she exclaimed! I love your accent!' A humorous incident, but a reminder of our ceaseless craving to either talk or listen to either talk or listen to music, lest we be left alone with our thoughts!

It was in the quietness of the temple, while Samuel was asleep, that the Lord spoke to him and called him - 'Samuel! Samuel!' It woke the lad and he obviously thought the old Priest needed him. But Eli had not called the child, it was God. The lad's ear was open and he heard the Lord speaking to him. I believe from that moment, Samuel was linked to divinity and then as David instructs us in Psalm, 91, 'He who chooses as his permanent abode, the dwelling place of the most high, shall always be in touch with the almightiness of God' (old Arabic translation of Psalm 91:1).

Young Samuel was now in touch with God and miracles were about to happen! The second point worth noting is 'The Samuel Knowledge'.

The knowledge was a revelation, not attained by an education system or a legal system of government - It was a divine revelation! God was going to judge the nation of Israel. The results were devastating!

The story is a reminder of the fact that God will ultimately judge the nation who rebels against His laws and introduces laws that God forbids. He declares that righteousness exalts a nation, but sin is a reproach to any nation. A study of history shows the results of God's judgment on individuals who knowingly and repeatedly ignore His laws. Are we seeing something of that today across our world? We need 'The Samuel Knowledge' to be aware of what is happening and to pray and prepare for the Lord's judgment. We need to be 'salt and light' whatever the cost!

'The Samuel Intuition' is what I have called his understanding of God's plan for His people. It is remarkable that a lad so young was able to discover the mind of God and know that judgment was on the way. His intuition and understanding of God's plan was accurate and subsequent events proved his predictions true. Recently, I overheard a conversation between two ladies. One said she was going to a fortune teller in a nearby city and related how others had been told things - some totally ridiculous prediction that had not come to pass! I compare that to young Samuel's intuition - His was from God! Fortune tellers get their information from Satan and therefore should be avoided at all times. Their father is the devil! Our Heavenly Father is the God who conquered the devil by raising His son, Jesus Christ from the dead and triumphed over sin. Ultimately, God will give Satan his final blow, when he will be chained in the lake of fire! We can and should claim victory over such power and seek to 'avoid the very appearance of evil'! Listen to what God has to say and He will honour and bless you!

A Prayer

Spirit of love and grace divine
Well up in this dry soul of mine,
All hardness chasing,
Proud self effacing,
Until my will is lost in Thine.

Spirit of truth and mighty power
Break the long drought with blessed shower,
Cleansing and filling,
With new life thrilling,
Decking each branch with fruit or flower.   Jean Corbett

Chosen and Special

READING   Deuteronomy 10: 12-22

'The Lord delighted only in your fathers,
to love them; and He chose their descendants after them,
you above all peoples, as it is this day.'   *Deuteronomy 10: 15*

We cannot explain God's reason for choosing Israel. But we do know that the founder of the nation was a godly man. Abraham proved his commitment to God by his faith - he believed God and it was accounted to him for righteousness. He proved his obedience by leaving Ur of the Chaldees and setting off not knowing where he was going. All Abraham knew was that he was obeying God, rather than man, whatever the cost. Abraham's other big plus for being so special was that he was called 'the friend of God'.

In the seed of Isaac and Jacob, God's favour continued. It was in Jacob, we see God's special favour extended towards this race. When Jacob, who was 'a deceiver' and the most unlikely candidate on whom a holy God would set His favour, met with God and wrestled all night, God changed His name to Israel, and thus the nation was born.

Tracing the history of Israel brings a greater surprise, but also an amazing revelation. Rahab was a harlot, Ruth was a non-Jew and David sinned grievously in the sight of God, yet they were chosen to be the ancestors of the Saviour of the world - the Lord Jesus Christ. We cannot explain it, but even in these three special people we can see the mercy of God to plan and bring salvation to 'the vilest offender, who truly believes' - He extended His grace and mercy to the Gentiles. No race or creed is excluded and no mater how vile the sinner, God's grace is extended towards him! Those who have been brought into the family of God thank Him for rescuing us and setting our feet on the solid Rock. What a rich inheritance! Thank God, despite our sin and utter unworthy state, God has reconciled us unto Himself and made us 'heirs with God and joint heirs with Christ'. Whatever happens in this life, we are safe! That is how special we are to God! No wonder we sing - 'I'm so glad I am part of the family of God!'

As God's chosen children, we must take seriously His commands and instructions. Therefore, let us examine these verses in Deuteronomy chapter ten. God says to His special people and to you and me...

'...what does the Lord your God require of you, but to fear the Lord your God, to walk in all His ways and to love Him, to serve the Lord your God with all your heart and with all your soul.

'and to keep the commandments of the Lord and His statutes which I command you today, for your good?' Deuteronomy, 10: 12 & 13.

Then Moses gives a list of ways in which to obey God's commands - be stiff-necked no longer; love the stranger; fear the Lord; serve Him; hold fast and take oaths in His name.

There is an awesome declaration in this chapter -

'For the Lord your God is God of gods and Lord of lords, the great God, mighty and awesome, who shows no partiality nor takes a bribe.' Deuteronomy 10:17. The closer we look at these words, the more challenging they become. To gain God's favour, we cannot give Him anything - not even our service. Not even giving financially to the work of God can help our acceptance, for He accepts no bribes. This Old Testament principle is carried into the era of Grace, for God's salvation cannot be paid for - it was paid by the Lord Jesus when He died on the Cross. Whatever we give to God and whatever we do for Him must be out of gratitude and must never be in order to gain merit and favour with Him. It is in mercy God deals with us and 'all our righteousness is as filthy rags' in His sight.

Pause in His presence today and give Him thanks for His goodness. Thank Him for selecting you and leading you to repentance and faith. Thank Him for bringing you into His family and ask for strength to reflect His image to a lost world.

God's Poem

You are God's poem, created in Christ
to be part of His nature and reflect His light:
Made in His image but marred by The Fall -
You were the reason that Christ gave His all!
He bore the sin that you might be free
when forsaken by God He hung on The Tree!

You are God's poem, a gift to His Son
to walk in communion with God's chosen One:
Sealed with the Spirit, you're now set apart -
you are a message to those in the dark!
Look at the harvest of grain that is ripe
for you, as God's reaper, to work until night!

You are God's poem, written and read,
sharing His bounty with those who need fed:
People are hurting with no friend to share -
they need understanding and someone to care!
Show that you love them and want to be part
of a deep inner healing God's Spirit will start!

You are God's poem, inspired by His love,
your name is engraved by your Father above
on the palms of His hands each letter's
    inscribed,
so why should you fear with Him at your side?
He knows the future whatever the test
and promises to be there to give you
    THE BEST!

'For we are His workmanship, created in Christ Jesus for good works, which God prepared beforehand that we should walk in them' Ephesians 2: 10.
(Note: The word translated 'workmanship,' is the same Greek word for 'poem'.)

Matchless Mercy

READING   Luke 23: 39-43

'And we indeed justly, for we receive the due reward
of our deeds; but this man has done nothing wrong'.   Luke 23: 41

*T*hree criminals are before the crowd on Golgotha -One is there accused of something He did not commit; the other two are there because they are thieves. The central cross holds the Son of God who came to earth to 'give His life a ransom for many' and on either side are two men who had done deeds that demanded justice and punishment. Look at the attitude of the Saviour. He is only interested in the eternal destiny of the two beside Him, while one of the other two, takes the attitude of self-defiance - 'If you are the Christ, save yourself and us'! His request indicates that he is a godless man.

The attitude of the other is total dependence on the mercy of God. He says, 'Do you not even fear God, seeing you are under the same condemnation?' He went on to elaborate by saying that the two of them were receiving their just rewards - in other words, they deserved it, but Jesus Christ had done nothing wrong. He was innocent! He then acknowledges Him as Lord and cries for mercy. 'Lord, remember me when you come into Your kingdom.' What trust rings out in these final words of a dying man!

Thus we see on Golgotha three individuals awaiting the death penalty - Jesus, the Messiah, a God-fearing criminal and a Godless criminal with no thought of his eternal destiny. It is interesting to note that the last person to repent and find forgiveness was a criminal. It reminds us of the mercy of God not only to the self-righteous but also to the sinner. No matter how low one has gone into the depths of sin, the Saviour can lift him from the miry clay and establish the truly penitent sinner on the solid rock, Christ Jesus. Truly this is matchless grace that is beyond measure.

When involved in evangelism in a southern Irish town, I took my team into a republican estate. It was obvious by the slogans that some of those who lived there were hardened criminals. With a certain amount of fear and trepidation, I knocked on each door. Nobody was rude or challenged me, despite my northern accent. One dear lady delayed me and cried pitifully, 'Can God forgive a murderer'? I assumed either a son or a close relative must have been involved in sectarian violence and been responsible for a murder. Thank God we have such a message of hope. One is able to give illustrations such as the great leader of Israel, Moses, who murdered an Egyptian and received God's pardon and forgiveness, or Pilate, who although he tried to wash his hands of any blame, was guilty of the death of the Son of God.

The Gospel gives hope to the hopeless, and wipes the slate clean. It also gives the repentant sinner, the power to 'go and sin no more'.

Benediction

Mercy be yours in abundance,
Mercy as deep as the sea,
Mercy as high as the heavens
Flowing from Mount Calvary.

Peace be yours in abundance,
Peace like a soft-falling dew,
Peace passing all understanding
God's benediction on you.

Love be yours in abundance
Love that is precious and pure,
Love to strengthen and sweeten
Love guaranteed to endure.

Jean Corbett

Watching for One Hour

READING   Mark 14: 32-42

'Simon, are you sleeping? Could you not watch one hour?'   *Mark 14: 37*

*A*ll four Gospels record the events leading up to the death of Christ. Each writer reveals certain events that had obviously left lasting impressions on his mind: but together, under the divine inspiration of the Holy Spirit, they give us a detailed account of the life of the Lord Jesus prior to the atonement. Luke records that 'He steadfastly set His face to go to Jerusalem.' Luke 9: 51. Jesus knew that He had come to fulfill the Father's will and to 'give His life a ransom for many', so this meant Jerusalem and eventual death on a cross.

The scene in Gethsemane comes immediately after His teaching session on faith, through the parable of the 'Fig Tree'; on respect for holy things, through the 'Cleansing of the Temple'. Then He follows with direct teaching on 'Forgiveness and Prayer' and 'The Second Coming'. He concludes His teaching by telling them to 'watch'. Because He was God, He knew they would fail, but He longed for them to be faithful to the end. One can almost hear His heart cry as He repeats again –'And what I say to you, I say to all, WATCH.' Mark 14: 37. Tragically, He uses the same word in the next chapter – 'Could you not WATCH one hour?'

When Jesus and the twelve came to Gethsemane, it seems they all entered the garden with its huge olive trees and tranquil atmosphere. Jesus leaves nine of them but takes Peter, James and John and goes a little farther. He then leaves these three in order to pray and face the battle of Calvary alone. He knew it would be a fierce conflict, so he urges them to watch.
'My soul is exceedingly sorrowful, even unto death, stay here and watch.'
When He returned the first time, he found the three asleep and said, 'Could you not watch with me one hour.? The second time he returned, again He found them asleep and repeated the question. The final time He came to the twelve and found them all asleep. It was too late for them, and as subsequent events proved – they failed in the hour of temptation! He wakened them and said, 'Arise, let us go!' What a sad moment for the Son of God! His trusted followers failed at the eleventh hour and utterly failed at the strike of the mid-night hour when "they all forsook Him and fled" and even Peter denied His Lord three times.

One of the many lessons to be learned from this account of Gethsemane is that if we do not pray, we are open to failure in the hour of testing.

Try Again

Try again –

    When you strike the wrong note
    and tears almost choke:
    When the music is blurred –
    Try again!

Try again –

    When you say the wrong thing
    and feel sadness within:
    When you feel a deep hurt –
    Try again!

Try again –

    When you let your Lord down
    and in prayer you feel bound:
    When the heavens are as brass –
    Try again!

Try again –

    When you give of your best
    and no one is blessed:
    When your service seems lost –
    Try again!

No Problems – Just Plans

READING   John 14: 1-7   Mark 13: 7.

'Let not your heart be troubled...'   *John 14: 1*

*A*re you troubled today?

It could be you are unnecessarily concerned about your health, old age, financial worries, family, society and the growing violence and sin around us. It could be you have had a bereavement in your family recently. What concerns you today? What is causing you to worry? Jesus taught us that it is wrong to worry.

To those who were worried about what they would wear, He used the illustration of the lily.
'Consider the lilies of the field how they grow: they neither toil, nor spin:' Matthew 6:28.

To further teach His disciples about worry, Jesus used an illustration we would all be familiar with - the grass.
'Now if God so clothes the grass of the field, which today is, and tomorrow is thrown into the oven, will He not much more clothe you , O you of little faith?' Matthew 6: 30.

Despite such exhortation from the Saviour, it is easy to be caught up with the cares of this life and allow worry to catch us unawares. Let's face the problem of health! With the ageing process come aches and pains, which we can expect. Much has been done in our world to help us cope with pain. God has favoured us to live in a country where more and more medication is available, and free for the aged - we are grateful for such blessings!

As Christians, we remember the suffering of the Lord Jesus Christ and take encouragement from His attitude to suffering - the only time He questioned God's will was in Gethsemane when He prayed,
'And He said, Abba, Father, all things are possible for You. Take this cup away from Me; nevertheless, not what I will, but what You will.' Mark 14: 36.

No one enjoys suffering and the best way to handle it is to tell the Lord about it and share your burden with your trusted friends so that they can pray for you. Don't take the burdens of your future health and bring them into the present. If you do, you will begin to worry, and the scriptures teach us that it is wrong to worry.

What about the worry of 'old age'? Again, we should cross that bridge when we reach it. God will look after us.

'I have been young, and now am old: yet have not seen the righteous forsaken, nor his descendants begging bread' - Psalm 37: 2 5.

Surely the God who cared for David in old age (it is generally accepted that this Psalm was written by David when he was old), will care for us!

Financial worries? This can bring unnecessary strain to some, but God has promised to provide for us and we can trust Him. This is more of a problem in countries where there is no 'Welfare State', and it is up to the more prosperous countries to help those less fortunate in this situation. Perhaps we should be considering ways in which we can do more for the 'stranger' and 'foreigner' in our own country!

Parents and Grandparents worry about their offspring. Again, it is time enough to worry when disaster strikes. It brings unnecessary pain to us when we 'cross our bridges before we come to them'. Let's leave it with the Lord and trust Him to look after our children and grandchildren. He will give the grace when the time comes, but not before it!

Society and all the ills! Yes, that would give us cause for concern. But again we cannot change it over-night, and we just have to pray that God will work His great purposes out for our fallen world. In fact, it must be expected that things can only get worse. Mark, in his Gospel, warns us that our world is heading for disaster. We have only to switch on the news to discover that -'it's later than we think!' But Jesus reassures us - '

'and when you hear of wars and rumours of wars, do not be troubled; for such things must happen, but the end is not yet'. Mark 13: 7.

Earthquakes, famines and flooding in various parts of the world have been caused by man's greed. God never intended us to destroy His world, but when Adam and Eve sinned in the Garden of Eden, sin began to destroy the natural world and as sin has increased on the earth, so has the pollution. We cannot blame God; it is the result of our own greed and destruction to something God made beautiful! The scriptures would encourage us to lend a helping hand in all such situations and help to alleviate suffering when within our power to do so. We should continue to pray for the victims of such natural disasters.

WHEN IS IT RIGHT TO WORRY?

The only thing we should be worried about is the SALVATION OF OUR SOULS. Corrie ten Boom, who hid Jews from the Nazis in the last war, suffered in a concentration camp and lost four of her family. She was able to forgive her enemies and lived a long and fruitful life to tell the world of the suffering she and the others experienced. She wrote to the two Gestapo soldiers who betrayed her family and told them she had forgiven them. One wrote back and said that if their family could show such love, and Jesus Christ could forgive him, he was accepting Him as his Saviour - the other was defiant and wrote expressing his regret that he had not killed more Jews. Such was the response of the two criminals who were crucified on either side of the Lord Jesus Christ. Do you know Him as your Saviour and friend? Both those Gestapo soldiers were executed one week after writing to Corrie - one, if he genuinely repented, has gone to be with Christ and the other is lost eternally.

*Eternity

When you have counted every grain
of sand from shore to shore:
Then climbed each hill and mountain peak
and lands beyond explored:
When you have dried all fallen tears,
mended each broken heart -
of the countless years of eternity
it will only be the start!

When you have counted all the stars
of heaven from east to west
and walked all roads and mountain trails -
yes, taking time to rest!
When you have brought a million smiles
to people, worlds apart -
of the countless years of eternity
it will only be the start!

* This poem is dedicated to my niece, Lynn, whom the Lord called Home five years ago at thirty three years of age. No matter how many poems I wrote, this was always Lynn's favourite. She is now enjoying her Saviour's presence - 'With Christ, which is far better!'

It is finished

READING   John 17: 1-5 and John 19: 28-37

'I have finished the work which You gave Me to do.'   *John 17 : 4*
'It is finished.'   *John 19 : 30*

*T*he life of Jesus spanned a mere thirty-three years, yet He accomplished more than any other person. Think of all the miracles He performed; His ministry to the sick and sorrowing; His encounters with individuals that resulted in what we would term a counselling ministry; the seasons of prayer alone and with His disciples; His training of the twelve; His friendship to the lonely. Ultimately the climax of His work was when He procured salvation for mankind. What a life!

Dr Martyn Lloyd Jones of Westminster Chapel said, "There is nothing so hopeless in the world... as the bankruptcy of the non-Christian view of life." Charles Darwin confessed at the end of his life that he had lost the power to enjoy poetry and music and, to a large extent, even the power to appreciate nature itself. The end of HG Wells was very similar. The title of his last book - 'Mind at The End of its Tether' reveals something of his turmoil.

The words of rationalist, Dr Marrett, head of a college in Oxford, could be added to a long list of eminent scholars who have left on record the emptiness of a barren life - "But to me the war brought to a sudden end the long summer of my life. Henceforth I have nothing to look forward to but chill autumn and still chillier winter, and yet I must somehow try not to lose heart." Many try to relieve themselves in their former successes and triumphs. For those who leave God out of their lives, the future is dark, but 'the path of the just is as a shining light, that shines more and more unto the perfect day.' Proverbs 4 :18

Jesus Christ is the perfect example of a life fulfilled and the course finished. As we view His life, death and resurrection we re-echo His own words from the Cross - "It is finished!"

Finished

A cross of wood,
    A leaden sky,
A vanquished foe,
    A victor's cry -
    "Finished!"

An open door,
    An empty tomb,
A glory chasing
    All the gloom -
    "Finished!"

A contrite heart,
    A promise sure,
A covenant
    That will endure -
    "Finished!"

Jean S Corbett

Awesome Wonder!

READING   Psalm 46

'God is our refuge and strength,
A very present help in trouble.
Therefore we will not fear, even though the earth be removed...
Though its waters roar and be troubled...'   Psalm 46: 1, 2a & 3a

The majestic Iguassu Falls, featured on the front cover of Daily Gems of Truth, forms a 2,700 metre horseshoe between Argentina and Brazil. Situated at the north of the province of Misiones, Argentina, and the most southerly cul-de-sac land area of Cascavel, Brazil, it is listed among the world's Natural Wonders. Standing close to the falls, the sound of millions of gallons of water thundering over the falls and crashing over the seventy two metre high falls, is deafening. Its waters roar! The explosive sound is frightening and its majesty is awesome! When I lived in Argentina, I had always hoped that one day I would visit the Iguassu Falls, but the demands of my work did not permit such a treat. Friends described them so vividly that I thought I could picture the scene, but when I visited the great Niagara Falls in Canada, I knew that videos, photographs, magazines, books and verbal descriptions could never convey the true picture of such gigantic water falls! It took the colour and reflections of the water as it fell, painting an indelible picture on my mind of wonder and amazement; the roar of the thunderous water crashing, as it were, to its death; it took the width of the entire falls, with tons of water spraying upwards wetting our faces as we sailed underneath the falls on 'The Maid of the Mist'; the horseshoe curve with a rainbow reflecting its colour and splendour on the water: it was the visual and audio effect that gave an emotional sensation - never to be forgotten! How I would have longed to be an artist to be able to paint my first panoramic view of the Niagara Falls!

Someone said to Turner, the renown English artist, I don't see in nature what you put into your pictures!' He replied, 'Don't you wish you could?'

Did David have a waterfall in mind when he wrote the third verse of this beautiful Psalm? Certainly, he was thinking of something bigger than Israel, in Psalm 46, for he writes about 'the earth', and in verse six, he writes about 'nations' and 'kingdoms'. What an amazing insight, before the age of exploration into the many regions beyond the lands of the Bible! Another proof of the infallible and inspired word of God!

This Psalm has brought comfort to the bereaved and suffering: it has been used to help the troubled: it has lifted the fallen and bound up the broken hearted: it has given strength to the fainting and brought hope to the dying.

Read it prayerfully. Dwell on the majesty of God in His awesome creation. Then focus on the things that give you concern today. In this Psalm, David deals with fear, weakness, trouble, the frightening roar of rushing water and earthquakes, hatred between nations, and war. Then, in verse ten, the troubled waters become still, as he quietens his readers with those soothing words -

'Be still and know that I am God;
I will be exalted among the nations.
I will be exalted in the earth!'

Finally, he lifts our thoughts to the 'Lord of hosts' and 'the God of Jacob'.
'The Lord of hosts is with us; The God of Jacob is our refuge.'

Sunrise

The fool has said within his heart
　　that God does not exist,
that man evolved from nothing -
　　creation is a myth!
but when I see the sunrise
　　dispel the morning mist -
I know that someone planned it:
I know that God exists!

He is a Master Artist
　　who paints the morning sky,
blends yellow, pink and orange
　　with grey and purple dye:
It changes every second
　　with ecstatic bursts of life
'till darkened lifeless shadows
are lost in morning light!

Life is a Journey

READING   John 14: 1-6 & Revelation 21: 1-8

*'Then I John, saw the holy city, New Jerusalem, coming down
out of heaven from God, prepared as a bride adorned for her husband...
'...there shall be no more death; nor sorrow,
nor crying. There shall be no more pain,
for the former things are passed away.'*   Revelation 21: 2 & 4b.

We do not need to be reminded that our journey through life will come to an end. The journey that began at birth will end at death - as far as the human body is concerned. But the scriptures teach us that for the soul, the grave is not the end - the soul of man will live as long as God lives. That means that spiritually we never had a beginning and will never have an end. Trillions of years from now, you and I will be alive!

It is important that we stop and take note of this fact, for soon we could make our last earthly journey and be face to face with our Maker.

The screech of brakes, the crunch of metal, the shriek of voices - voices that were chatting merrily in the back seat of a speeding sports car. Yes, you have guessed - another fatal accident!

As the ambulance speeds off and the police gather up pieces of crushed metal for examination, distraught onlookers unconsciously give vent to expressions or horror, sadness and pity. Whether as a result of a terminal illness, a fatal accident, a natural disaster, or just the cycle of life, one in one die! There is no escape from the clutches of man's last enemy, death! Each of us will have to leave behind our loved ones and the things that we are now familiar with, and go through 'the valley of the shadow of death'. It is the last journey we will take and one which demands the most preparation! We cannot take the risk of treating it like all other journeys in life.

Going on holiday, some people seem to be able to throw things into the case and go off without much preparation, but if there is a special function to attend to or an important person to meet, care has to be taken to put the proper clothing into the case - Preparation is a must for such a holiday.

The thing that is important about the last journey we will take, is that there may not be any time to prepare. The departure date could come unexpectedly! A fatal road accident is not planned - neither is a heart-attack, a stroke or a terminal illness. Take heed of God's warning voice and make sure you are ready for any emergency departure, otherwise it may be too late.

If you have made preparation for the journey into eternity, by repenting of sin and asking the Lord Jesus Christ to be your Saviour and Lord, you have nothing to fear - Your journey is Home!

Your place is 'prepared for you' by the Saviour. It is beyond anything you have ever imagined possible. There will be no pain and sickness there - no sorrow or crying! What a prospect for the child of God!

We should be happy for the believer who leaves us and whose spirit takes flight to 'realms of eternal day'. There will be no sorrow there!

Journey's End

When I am gone
   Sing no sad songs
For sadness to
   This world belongs,
But from your heart
   An anthem raise
Of joyous and
   Triumphant praise.

When I am gone
   Lay no wreaths there
For sun and storm
   to strip and bare,
But sow some seed
   Your faith to prove,
And let the flowering
   Be of love.

When I am gone
   Grieve not for me,
From cage of clay
   At last set free,
But peel the bells
   With gladsome lay
To speed my spirit
   On its way.

Jean Corbett

The Resurrection and the Life

READING   John 11: 1-44

'I am the resurrection and the life,
He who believes in Me, though he may die, he shall live'.   *John, 11: 25*

*I*n summing up the story of Easter, it has been aptly said, 'The resurrection is God's receipt that the price has been paid'. Without the resurrection, Jesus Christ would have gone down in history as a remarkable man, who healed the sick and went about doing good. No doubt He would have been remembered as the greatest man of the first century, whose remarkable miracles would have been recounted to succeeding generations and he would have taken his place with others that had contributed to the good of mankind. But Jesus Christ rose from the dead and is 'the first fruits of those who sleep'. He is alive! He is seated at the right hand of God and lives to make intercession for the believer. What an amazing fact!

The corn of wheat has fallen into the ground and died and for over two thousand years has been springing up to produce life. When Lazarus died, Jesus delayed coming in order that God might be glorified through Lazarus being raised from the dead. The death of Lazarus not only gave the opportunity to Jesus to perform a miracle but it also gave Him the opportunity to teach all present, and succeeding generations, the truth of the believer's immortality. Martha knew that truth for she said, 'I know that he will rise again in the resurrection'. It was in reply to this that Jesus said 'I am the resurrection and the life, He who believes in Me, though he may die, he shall live'. Embodied in the resurrection is this amazing and wonderful truth - the Christian will be raised and will be given a glorified body, like that of the Saviour. Not only is the resurrection of 'saints' a New Testament truth, but it is an Old Testament truth as well. The book of Job brings out this great fact - 'For I know that my Redeemer lives, and He shall stand at last on the earth: 'And after my skin is destroyed, this I know, that in my flesh I shall see God'. The greatest comfort anyone can bring to those who mourn is that there is life after death. It is a Biblical truth proclaimed throughout the pages of scripture and re-echoed down through the centuries. Let us rejoice in the resurrection and in the glorious prospect of life beyond the grave. As far as human life is concerned death is final, but not final as far as eternal life is concerned
- We shall rise again!

No Sting in Death

No sting in death
    For Christ has died
        To deal with sin and give you peace
            In Christ.

No sting in death
    So do not fear
        To cross the vale and wake to be
            With Christ.

No sting in death
    Just sleep my child
        So close your eyes and you'll awake
            In heaven.

No sting in death
    For Christ arose
        So be assured that you will be
            Glorified!

Are You Troubled?

READING   John 14: 1-7 & Mark 13: 3-13

'Let not your heart be troubled....'   *John 14: 1*

*A*re you troubled today? It could be you are unnecessarily concerned about your job, family, friends, future, health, old age, financial worries, our society and the growing violence and sin around us. What is causing you to worry? Jesus wants to lift your burden and carry it for you! But you must commit your way to Him!

To those who were worried about what they would wear, He used the illustration of the lily.

'So why do you worry about clothing? Consider the lilies of the field, how they grow: they neither toil nor spin;' Matthew 6: 28.

To further teach His disciples about worry, Jesus used an illustration everyone would be familiar with – the grass.

'Now if God so clothes the grass of the field, which today is, and tomorrow is thrown into the oven, will He not much more clothe you, O you of little faith?' Matthew 6: 30.

Do you fear the future? God has a plan for your life! If you have failed in one aspect of your career, there is still a plan – place your plans in God's hands and share your burden with a trusted friend and ask for prayer. Many young people have proved that God answers prayer about their career, so why not trust Him to open the right doors for you – then watch and wait for the answers! Have patience because when God says, 'wait' it is just as important as when He says 'Go'!

'I know your works. See, I have set before you an open door and no one can shut it...' Revelation 3: 8a.

Wait for the door to open!

Let's face the problem of health! With the ageing process, there comes aches and pains, and although we find it difficult to cope at times, we have the advantage of an excellent health system in most of our western civilization – a lot of pain can be alleviated today with new discoveries in pain relieving drugs. It is important to appreciate all that is available to us and make sure we do not take the burdens of our future health and bring them into the present. If we do, we shall certainly begin to worry. Ask God to help those who do not have access to pain relief.

What about the worry of 'old age'? When old age comes, God has promised to be with us. We should not try to cross that bridge until we reach it! God will look after us!

'I have been young, and now am old:
Yet have not seen the righteous forsaken,
Nor his descendants begging bread.' Psalm 37: 25.
Surely the God, who cared for David in old age, will care for us!
Financial worries? This can bring unnecessary stain to some, but God has promised to meet our needs.
Parents and Grandparents worry about their offspring. It brings pain to us when we 'cross our bridges before we come to them'. Let's leave it with the Lord and trust Him to look after our children! He will give the Grace when the time comes, but not before it.
Are you worried about society and all the ills? Yes, that would give us cause for concern, but we cannot change it over-night, therefore, it is better to pray that God will work His great purposes out for our fallen world - Look up for 'our God reigns'!

Be Careful for Nothing

'Be careful for nothing'
I heard Jesus say –
    as from life's rugged pathway
I took time to pray!
    'Your fears and your worries
I understand –
    they disappear at My command!'

'Be careful for nothing'
    I quickly replied
as with furrowed brow
    the Word I applied:
He showed me His promise –
    Yes! He understood!
The forces of evil
    He promptly withstood!

'Be careful for nothing'
    My motto shall be
as I press for the prize
    and His welcome to me.
With patience I'll serve Him -
    for He understands
my preparation for better lands!

God's Waiting Time

READING   Exodus 3: 1-22

'Now Moses was tending the flock of Jethro his father-in-law,
the priest of Midian. And he led the flock to the back of the desert,
and came to Horeb, the mountain of God.'   *Exodus 3: 1*

*W*hen God asks us to wait, it is because He has a purpose in mind that requires more training for us and more glory for Him. We do not always see God's purpose at the time and very often we rebel against Him, and those whom He uses, in the learning process.

We can learn lessons from some of the great Bible characters. Moses is a classic example of 'God's Waiting Time'. Moses had to learn lessons in the desert, before God could trust him to lead His people. I have no doubt, there were times when he did not understand God's purpose. After all, he could have been King in Egypt, but instead, he chose to suffer with the people of God rather than enjoy the wealth of the palace and all the pomp that came with such a life-style. God was first in His life! The outcome was - he became a humble shepherd for a large part of his life. Why? God had a purpose and Moses was the man God wanted to use for His plan for a nation and for the world. Moses may have questioned many times, as he whiled away the hours in the mountains around Horeb, but he discovered that 'in acceptance lies peace', and accepted the will of God.

Moses may not always have been a humble man, or a meek man - in fact his previous history as a murderer, proves that God had to remould the vessel and make it one that would bring honour and glory to His name, before He could trust him to lead His people. As a result, he developed into a great leader - after his preparation as a shepherd and his experience of God at the 'Burning Bush'. Prior to that he would have failed miserably in such a position. It took the daily routine of a shepherd, when he had ample time alone with his own thoughts and struggles to learn dependence on his God; it took the awesome encounter with a Holy God at the Burning Bush, to purify him and fit him for the great task ahead. The years of preparation were necessary for his future ministry!

Many of God's servants know the pruning Hand of God in their lives prior to attempting major tasks in the Lord's service. None of God's servants would say the preparation time was easy - but it was necessary!

God's Intricate Tapestry

If all our skies were sunny and all our mornings bright,
we would complain of dizziness, because of too much light.
There must be clouds and darkness, and haziness and rain -
there must be joy and laughter, to balance ache and pain.

If instant were our produce, like supermarket goods,
then farmers wouldn't know the joy of season's changing moods.
There wouldn't be the sowing, or waiting for the grain
to ripen in the sunshine, mature with warmth and rain.

If we had wealth and grandeur and never had to toil,
we would complain of boredom and from the world recoil.
There must be times of leanness, as well as times of fun -
It's knowing times of hardship, brings release when goals are won!

So waiting has a purpose and dark days play a part
in the intricacies of tapestry, designed by God's loving heart
to make life's burdens easy, and refine us as pure gold -
God makes 'vessels unto honour' in a very special mould!